Passenger to Teheran

Vita Sackville-West in 1925.

Passenger to Teheran

V. SACKVILLE-WEST

with a new introduction by

NIGEL NICOLSON

HarperPerennial

A Division of HarperCollins*Publishers*

Designed by Peter Guy

Library of Congress Cataloging-in-Publication Data

Sackville-West, V. (Victoria), 1892–1962.
    Passenger to Teheran / V. Sackville-West ; with a new introduction
by Nigel Nicolson. — 1st HarperPerennial ed.
        p.   cm.
    Originally published: London : Hogarth Press, 1926.
    ISBN 0-06-097458-3 (paper)
    1. Sackville-West, V. (Victoria), 1892–1962—Journeys—Iran.
2. Authors, English—20th century—Journeys—Iran.   3. Iran—
Description and travel.   I. Title.
    [DS258.S2   1992]
    915.504′52—dc20   91-58478

92 93 94 95 96 HC 10 9 8 7 6 5 4 3 2 1

CONTENTS

ILLUSTRATIONS

MAPS

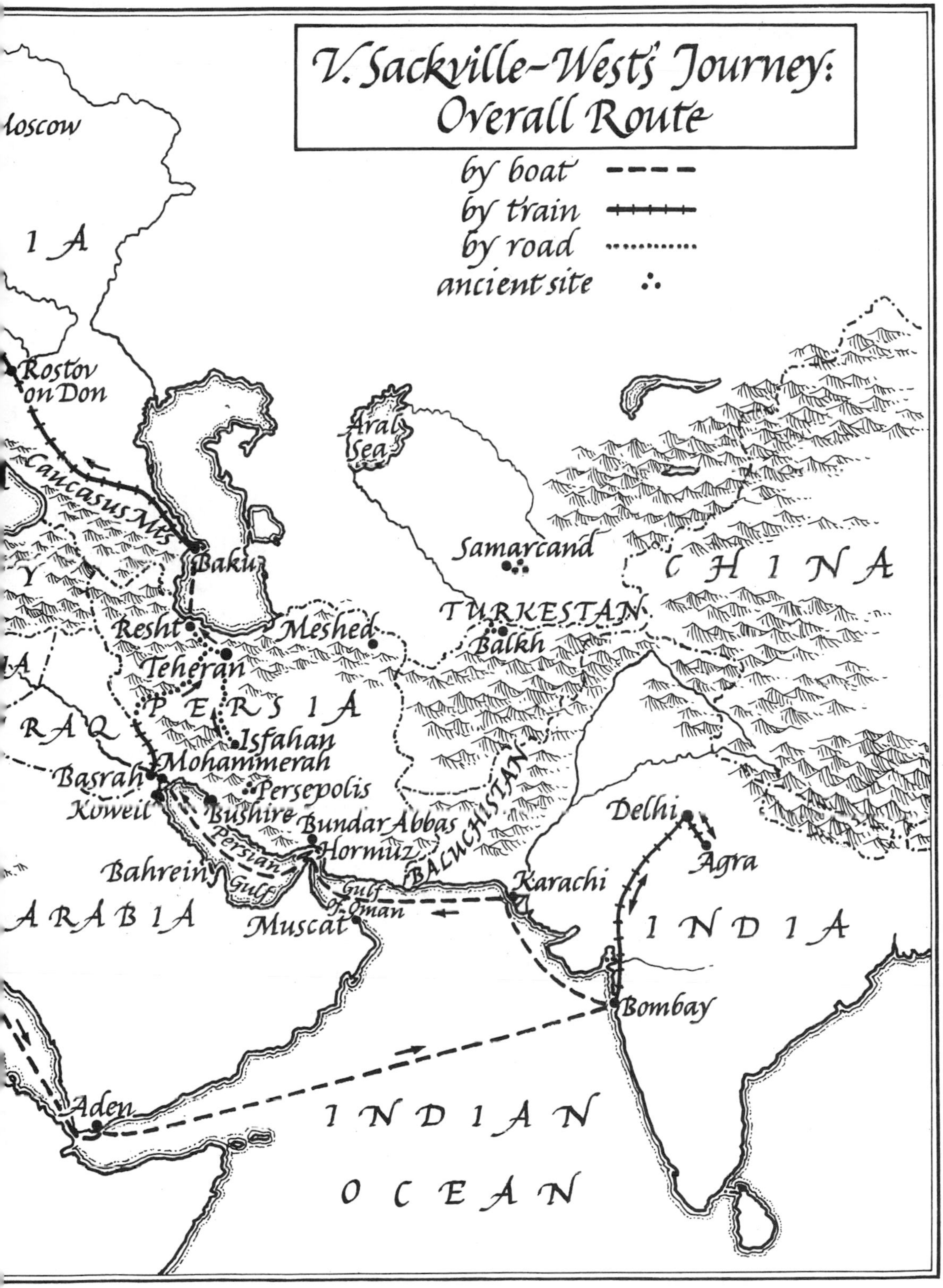

V. Sackville-West's Journey:
Overall Route

by boat - - - - -
by train +++++
by road ....
ancient site ∴

Moscow

I A

Rostov
on Don

Caucasus Mts

Baku

Aral
Sea

Samarcand

C H I N A

TURKESTAN

Resht   Meshed
Teheran   Balkh

P E R S I A

RAQ   Isfahan
Basrah   Mohammerah
Koweit   Persepolis

Bushire   Bundar Abbas
Bahrein   Hormuz

BALUCHISTAN

Delhi

Agra

Karachi

Persian
Gulf

Gulf
of Oman

I N D I A

ARABIA

Muscat

Bombay

Aden

I N D I A N

O C E A N

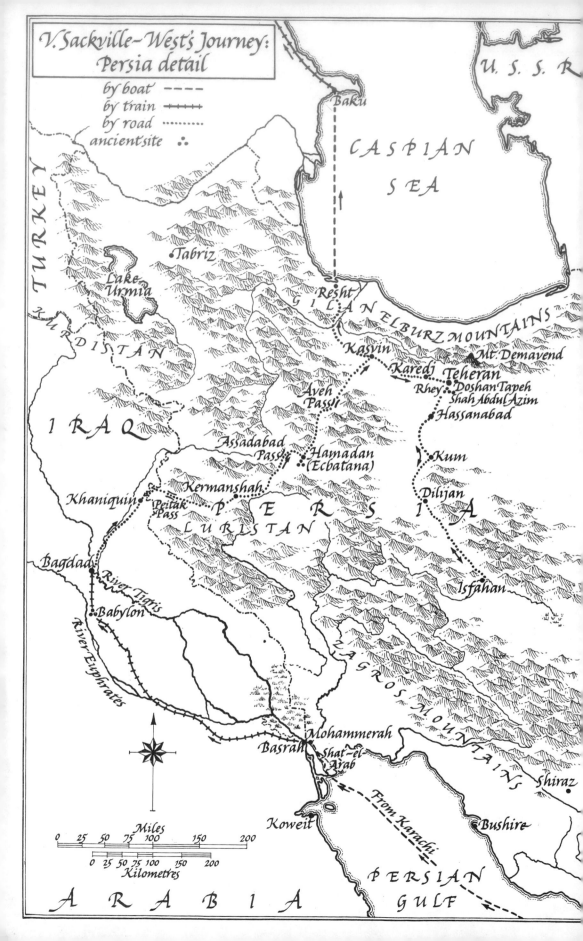

V. Sackville-West's Journey:
Persia detail

by boat - - - - -
by train ++++++
by road ·········
ancient site ∴

U. S. S. R.

Baku

CASPIAN
SEA

TURKEY

·Tabriz

Lake
Urmia

KURDISTAN

Resht

GILAN
ELBURZ MOUNTAINS

Kasvin

Mt. Demavend

Karedj Teheran

Rhey· ·Doshan Tapeh
Shah Abdul Azim

Aveh
Pass

·Hassanabad

IRAQ

Assadabad
Pass

Hamadan
(Ecbatana)

·Kum

Kermanshah·

·Dilijan

Khaniquin

Peitak
Pass

P E R S I A

L U R I S T A N

·Isfahan

Bagdad

River Tigris

·Babylon

Z A G R O S   M O U N T A I N S

River Euphrates

Mohammerah

Basrah· Shat-el-
Arab

·Shiraz

From Karachi

Koweit

·Bushire

Miles
0 25 50 75 100   150   200

0 25 50 75 100   150   200
Kilometres

A R A B I A

P E R S I A N
GULF

VITA Sackville-West began her book of Persian travels with the provocative statement, "There is no greater bore than the travel bore", and then, by her account of her own journey, disproves it. *Passenger to Teheran* is utterly different from a returned traveller's lecture, with slides, to a suffering audience of his friends. It gives pleasure because it describes pleasure, illuminated by what Winifred Holtby called in a contemporary review of the book, "the lucid tranquillity of her lovely prose".

The author is eloquent about her adventures and reactions, and it would be easy to trace her route on a map, but she is reticent to the point of obscurity about her own identity, her companions on different parts of the journey and her motives for it. If one did not know that the 'V' of her name stood for Victoria, abbreviated by family and friends to Vita, one could be left uncertain of her sex until the very last page when she confesses, "The customs-house officer at the Dutch frontier made me an offer of marriage." It is evident that she did not always travel alone, but the other half of 'we' is never identified. She speaks of diplomatic parties without saying that her husband was HM's Counsellor in Teheran, of letter-writting without revealing that her chief correspondent was Virginia Woolf, and of her 'work' without adding that she was completing in Persia her long poem *The Land* which is still her greatest literary testament.

In the Introduction to a new edition, published more than sixty years after the first, it is legitimate, I hope, to explain circumstances which she chose to suppress.

Vita's husband, Harold Nicolson, had won an early reputation in the Foreign Office as one of the most brilliant of its young diplomatists, becoming the pet of successive Foreign Secretaries, Balfour and Curzon, and was engaged at this very moment in writing his best-remembered book *Some People*. He was posted to the Legation in Teheran in November 1925 as the second-ranking officer in a small diplomatic team which included Sir Percy Loraine as Minister and Gladwyn Jebb as a young 3rd Secretary. Vita refused to accompany her husband to Teheran where she would be regarded as a resident wife without any other qualification (hating to be Mrs Nicolson when she could be Vita Sackville-West, writing, gardening, at Long Barn in the Weald), but she visited him twice, because she loved him and liked the idea of Persia for its remoteness and lack of sophistication, first in 1926, the journey which this book describes, and again in the next year, when she walked with him over the Bakhtiari Mountains, an expedition

Harold Nicolson with doves at Long Barn, Harold and Vita's home near Sevenoaks, Kent. The building on the left is the original 14th-century farmhouse. Harold added the other wing in 1916, using timbers of an old barn which lay below the garden and gave the house its name.

which formed the substance of her second book of Persian travels,
Twelve Days.

She left England on 20 January 1926 and returned in mid-May. Her journey was circuitous and leisurely, partly from choice because she had never seen India or Iraq before, and partly because travel in the Middle East by sea and land was still almost medieval in its sluggishness. Vita was accompanied as far as India by her intimate friend, the poet Dorothy Wellesley. Together they mounted the Nile as far as Luxor, and in India visited Agra and New Delhi. Vita then continued alone, by sea up the Persian Gulf, by rail to Bagdad where she stayed a few days with Gertrude Bell, and then overland by a trans-desert convoy of cars to the Persian mountains and onwards to Teheran.

It is striking how much she omits from her narrative. There is no mention of Dorothy Wellesley, much to the latter's fury. Ecstatic as Vita was about the Valley of the Kings, she made no reference to what she undoubtedly knew and saw, that Howard Carter was in the third year of his excavation of Tutenkhamun's tomb. She allows India no more than a page, disliking it. "A loathsome place", she wrote to Virginia Woolf, "without one shred of any quality, and I never want to go there again", and didn't.

> "Jungle on either side of the train", she explained to Virginia, "rocks looking like medieval castles; peacocks paddling in the village pond. Roads tracked in the dust, seen from train windows, leading where? A jackal staring in the scrub. An English General. The Taj Mahal like a pure and sudden lyric. And everywhere squalor, squalor, squalor. Children's eyes black with flies. Men with sores. Mangy dogs. Filthy hovels not fit for pigs. And a bridge that was a concourse of men and animals and carts, all shoving, huddling, shouting, as our motor clove its way through like a snow-plough. Noise and squalor, squalor and noise, everywhere."

Her meeting with her old friend Edwin Lutyens on the site of his half-built Viceregal house in New Delhi merits only half a line. She conceals from the reader her never-forgotten meeting with Harold at Kermanshah where he awaited her (his diary says) "in a terrible state of impatience, anxiety and excitement", and Vita arrived, perfectly composed after a four-day bandit-ridden journey over the Persian mountains with a saluki hound across her knees.

One would not know from her account that they lived in the Counsellor's house in the compound of the British Legation in Teheran, the very place where Harold was born in 1886, when his father was Minister. By Persian standards it was quite comfortable. They had four servants, a stable of horses and the small fleet of Legation Fords at their command. Vita could spend part of most days as she wished, in the bazaars or in search of wild plants in the near-desert that surrounded the city, but she did her duty, however reluctantly, as the Counsellor's wife, attending parties which tried to reproduce in the alien atmosphere of Central Asia the diplomatic civilities of Western capitals, and they bored her extremely. More for Harold's sake than for his colleagues' she suppressed her *ennui* in the book, but it spilled into her letters to Virginia:

> "Compound life means that at 8 a.m. the Consul's son aged ten starts an imitation of a motor horn; that at 9 a.m. someone comes and says have I been letting all the water out of the tank; that at 10 a.m. the Military Attaché's wife strolls across and says how are your delphiniums doing; that at 11 a.m. Lady Loraine appears and says wasn't it monstrous the way the Russian Ambassador's wife cut the Polish Chargé d'Affaires' wife last night at the Palace; that at 12 noon a gun goes off and the muezzins of Teheran set up a wail for prayer; that at 1 p.m. it is time for luncheon, and Vita hasn't done any work."

She minded most the indifference of the uprooted Europeans to Persia itself. They thought, and complained, only of its inefficiencies and discomforts, blinkered to the beauty of the country, the gentleness of its people, its gardens, literature and art. Persia had not welcomed since Curzon a more observant and appreciative British visitor than Vita. If the Persians are cruel to animals, she tells us, it is because they are "ignorant of suffering". If she feels momentarily homesick, "sitting on a rock, with the yellow tulips blowing all about me and a little herd of gazelles moving down in the plain, I dwell with a new intensity on my friends". When people complain that the uplands are bleak, Vita is consoled by "the light, and the space, and the colour that sweeps in waves, like a blush over a proud and sensitive face". Persia is full of life for those who take the trouble to seek it, "tiny, delicate and shy, escaping the broader glance", and she was not thinking only of a gentian hiding in the shadow of a rock. She could endow these limitless plains with the personality of the humble goatherd, or the goat itself, which slowly crossed it.

From Teheran she made only one major expedition this year, to Isfahan. Harold came with her and, though she does not mention him except by the collective "we", Raymond Mortimer, Harold's intimate friend. They travelled through an almost deserted country in a battered car trussed with their luggage like a dromedary, slept in bare rooms and ate tinned food for want of any other thing digestible. The most eloquent section of *Passenger to Teheran* is Vita's description of this trip. With admirable economy she conveys the impression of the road leading on and on to regions ever more remote, with never a suspicion that she wished she had not come. She was a born traveller, with that rare capacity to love equally two such different places as her native Kentish Weald and the bare uplands of Persia which looked to her no different than once to Alexander or Genghis Khan. Virginia Woolf, on receiving her

Virginia Woolf photographed by Vita at Monk's House, Rodmell, in Sussex. She was Vita's most intimate friend at the time of the Persian journey, and their correspondence supplements Vita's published account of it.

letters, wrote in her diary, "She is not clever: but abundant and fruitful, truthful too. She taps so many sources of life: repose and variety."

Returning from Isfahan to Teheran Vita helped decorate the Gulestan Palace for the coronation of Reza Khan. The ceremony is one of the set-pieces of the book, Vita as a journalist, describing the Shah as a "Cossack trooper with a brutal jaw", which appalled Harold when the book was published, for this was the sovereign to whom he was accredited. She ends with her frightening journey home through Russia and Poland. This is Vita the adventuress and humorist. What she leaves out is the agony of her parting from Harold on the shores of the Caspian. Each felt that the absence of the other was not to be endured. But they were young, Vita 34, Harold 39, and they now had in common an experience which Vita immortalised in this book.

When Virginia Woolf read the typescript for publication by the Hogarth Press, she wrote to Vita, "It's awfully good.... I didn't know the extent of your subtleties ... not the sly, brooding, thinking, evading Vita. The whole book is full of nooks and crannies, the very intimate things one says in print", but not face to face, not even in letters. Indeed Virginia was startled by her "not clever" friend's lively, reflective prose, and one suspects, a trace jealous of it. *Passenger to Teheran* was written, so to speak, on the hoof, as she travelled. She could describe a scene, a person, an emotion with enviable spontaneity, plunging her hands into the treasury of the English language as greedily as into the jewel-chests of the Shah. It is a glittering book, like its contemporary *The Land*, both the product of her tumultuous maturity.

NIGEL NICOLSON
Sissinghurst
April, 1990

Passenger to Teheran

CHAPTER I

INTRODUCTORY

T R A V E L is the most private of pleasures. There is no greater bore than the travel bore. We do not in the least want to hear what he has seen in Hong-Kong. Not only do we not want to hear it verbally, but we do not want – we do not really want, not if we are to achieve a degree of honesty greater than that within the reach of most civilised beings – to hear it by letter either. Possibly this is because there is something intrinsically wrong about letters. For one thing they are not instantaneous. If I write home to-day and say (as is actually the fact), "At this moment of writing I am sailing along the coast of Baluchistan", that is perfectly vivid for me, who have but to raise my eyes from my paper to refresh them with those pink cliffs in the morning light; but for the recipient of my letter, opening it in England at three weeks' remove, I am no longer coasting Baluchistan; I am driving in a cab in Bagdad, or reading in a train, or asleep, or dead; the present tense has become meaningless. Nor is this the only trouble about letters. They do not arrive often enough. A letter which has been passionately awaited should be immediately supplemented by another one, to counteract the feeling of flatness that comes upon us when the agonising delights of anticipation have been replaced by the colder flood of fulfilment. Now when notes may be sent by hand, as between lovers living in the same town, this refinement of correspondence is easy to arrange, but when letters have to be transported by the complex and altogether improbable mechanism of foreign mails (those bags lying heaped in the hold!), it is impossible. For weeks we have waited; every day has dawned in hope (except Sunday, and that is a day to be blacked out of the calendar); it may have waned in disappointment, but the morrow will soon be here, and who knows what to-morrow's post may not bring? Then at last it comes; is torn open; devoured; – and all is over. It is gone in a flash, and it has not sufficed to feed our hunger. It has told us either too much or too little. For a letter, by its arrival, defrauds us of a whole secret region of our existence, the only region indeed in which the true pleasure of life may be tasted, the region of imagination, creative and protean, the clouds and beautiful shapes of whose heaven are destroyed by the wind of reality. For observe, that to hope for Paradise is to live in Paradise, a very different thing from actually getting there.

The poor letter is not so much in itself to blame, – and there is, I think, a peculiar pathos in the thought of the writer of that letter, taking pains, pouring on to his page so much desire to please, so human a wish to communicate something of himself, in his exile, – not so much to blame in the inadequacy of its content, as in the fact that it has committed the error of arriving, of turning up. "Le rôle d'une femme", said an astute Frenchman once, "est non de se donner, mais de se laisser désirer."

The art of reading letters, too, is at least as great as the art of writing them, and possessed by as few. The reader's co-operation is essential. There is always more to be extracted from a letter than at first sight appears, as indeed is true of all good literature, and letters certainly deserve to be approached as good literature, for they share this with good literature: that they are made out of the intimate experience of the writer, begotten of something personally endured. But it is not every one who knows how to read. Many a word, wrung out of the pen, many an indication, gets thrown on to the dust-heap because it stood alone, unamplified and unsupported. Only the ideal reader appreciates the poignancy of understatement.

Furthermore, to letters of travel attaches a special disability. The link between two persons must indeed be close before one of them is really eager to visualise the background against which the other moves; to see with his eyes, hear with his ears, be transplanted to the heat of his plains or the rigours of his mountains. If this link exist, well and good; and certainly it is a fine and delicate form of mental exercise to reconstruct a landscape, to capture so subtle a thing as the atmospheric significance of a place, from the indications given; rather, reconstruction and capture are words too gross for the lovelier unreality that emerges, a country wholly of the invention, like those roseate landscapes of the romantic Italian painters, but it is an art in itself, a luxury for the idle and speculative, repaid – with a freakish twist – when later on we tread with our mortal feet that place which for so long served as the imaginary country of our wanderings (for nothing is harder than to re-evoke a place as we knew it before we went there, so tenuous was the fabric of our weavings, so swiftly dispelled, for all its apparent solidity and its detail; as a place that we knew in childhood, now wrongly remembered in colour and size, under the fresh but not necessarily truer impression of our actual beholding). But if this stimulus be absent, then it is, let us confess it, with a weary conscientiousness that we read the descriptive passages of our nomad friends. Even those letters which were not addressed to us, nor to any of our generation, the letters of Beckford, let us say, or of Lady Mary Montagu, we read less for the sake of the countries described than for their historical curiosity (in itself an adventitious thing), or as we read a diary, for the strokes of vigour, humour, or downrightness which unconsciously build up the personality of the writer. "As a diary", in fact, is no bad comparison, for in a diary, even though compiled by the most illiterate of pens, that which stands out, in the ultimate and cumulative sense, is its

convincingness, investing, by its bald, gradual, and uncom-
promising method, even the dullest record with the indisputable
effect of truth.

There would seem, then, to be something definitely wrong about
all letters of travel, and even about books of travel, since the letters
of another age, collected into library editions, may fairly claim to
rank as books rather than as mere correspondence. There would
seem, going a step further, to be something wrong about travel
itself. Of what use is it, if we may communicate our experience
neither verbally nor on paper? And the wish to communicate our
experience is one of the most natural, though not one of the most
estimable, of human weaknesses. Not one of the most estimable,
for it is æsthetically unprofitable (since a pleasure shared is a
pleasure halved), and, as an attempt, in the last resort fallacious
(since no experience can ever be truly communicated, and the only
version we can hope to get through to another person but a garbled,
deceptive account of what really happened to us). Travel is in sad
case. It is uncomfortable, it is expensive; it is a source of annoyance
to our friends, and of loneliness to ourselves. Of course to the true
solitary this last is a great recommendation; but loneliness and
solitude are not even first cousins. The true solitary will savour his
apartness; he will feel that he is himself only when he is alone;
when he is in company he will feel that he perjures himself,
prostitutes himself to the exactions of others; he will feel that time
spent in company is time lost; he will be conscious only of his
impatience to get back to his true life. Alone, – for although he
may put on carpet slippers the furnishings of his mind are fastidious
in the extreme, – he will draw a book from his shelf, or from his
store of images some toy that delights him, rolling it round in his
mind as the gourmet a grape in his mouth, tasting the one sweet
escaped drop of its juice before he bursts it into its full flood against
his palate.

It may be that language, that distorted labyrinthine universe,
was never designed to replace or even to complete the much simpler
functions of the eye. We look; and there is the image in its entirety,
three-dimensional, instantaneous. Language follows, a tortoise
competing with the velocity of light; and after five pages of print
succeeds in reproducing but a fraction of the registered vision. It
reminds one of the Oriental who with engaging naivety thought
that by photographing the muezzin he would record also the notes
of his call to prayer. The most – but what a most! – that language
can hope to achieve is suggestion; for the art of words is not an
exact science. We do not indeed reflect often enough how strange
a world-within-the-world we have created by this habit of language, so strongly rooted in us by tradition and custom, so taken for
granted, that we are no longer capable of imagining life without
it, as one of those ideas which the mind is unable to conceive, like

the end of time or the infinity of space. Thought is impossible without words; and the process of thought appears to us a desirable exercise; but how are we to know what relation thought bears to the world of fact? whether any true relation at all, or merely a conventionalised, stylised relation such as is borne by art, that extraordinary phenomenon, that supreme paradox of conveying truth through various conventions of falsity? Such may well be the secure and presumptuous position of language, but since we are moving in a vicious circle, having no weapon against words but other words, it seems improbable that we shall ever be able to judge. It is said that the new-born child knows no emotion but that of fear induced by noise; consequently all other emotions, and all other ideas, must be the result of learning and association; but from the baby startled by the beating of a gong to the finest and most complicated product of the civilised brain is a terrifying road to travel. Give a thing a name, and it immediately achieves an existence; but either that thing had an existence before it had a name, or else the reverse is the case; we cannot tell which. Thus for the Hindu 'to-morrow' and 'yesterday' have but one denomination, so that we may assume his idea of relative time to be very different from our own, or surely he would have forged a word to suit the needs of his enlarged perceptions. We have no means of apprehending those ideas which we cannot clothe in words, any more than we are capable of imagining a form of life into which none of the elements already familiar to us should enter; yet it would be no more reasonable for us to pretend that such ideas may not exist, than for a child to crumple in a temper a handbook of higher mathematics. We are the slaves of language, strictly limited by our tyrant.

Moreover, the contradictions contained within the capacities of language are violent and astonishing. At one moment it seems that there is nothing (within the limits of our experience) that may not be expressed in words, down to the finest hair-stroke of a Proust or a Henry James; next moment we recognise in despair, so poor is our self-imposed vehicle, our incapacity truly to communicate to one another the simplest experience of our factual or emotional life. Who amongst us could boast that, transplanted into the mind of another person, even though that person be his nearest, he would not find himself in a strange country, recognising here and there a feature that he knew, but on the whole baffled by unexpected grouping, shape, and proportion? There is only one province of life with which language is almost fitted to deal: the province of the intellect, because that is the province, so to speak, begotten by language itself, which without language would never, could never, have come into existence. Those things which are felt, and those things which are seen, because they exist independently, and in no ratio to the degree of our articulateness, are not the business of words.

One must concede then, and sadly, that travel is a private pleasure, since it consists entirely of things felt and things seen, — of sensations received and impressions visually enjoyed. There is no intellectual interest in travelling, and most intellectuals have been stay-at-homes. They prefer, wisely perhaps, to doze by the gas fire and let the minarets and cupolas arise without risking the discouragement of disillusion. Or, more probably even, they never think of the minarets and cupolas at all, but root their interest in the stray, perplexing souls of their friends. Travel is simply a taste, not to be logically defended; nor standing in any need of defence, since it cannot be argued away, but remains there like a good concrete fact, not to be talked into nothingness, but sticking up as solidly when the mists of argument have cleared, as it did when their futile miasma began to arise. Nothing is an adventure until it becomes an adventure in the mind; and if it be an adventure in the mind, then no circumstance, however trifling, shall be deemed unworthy of so high a name. In common with all the irrational passions it has to be accepted; irritating it may be, but it is there.

And like all irrational passions it is exceedingly romantic. At first sight it would appear to be too materialistic for romance, being based on material things, such as geography, which is concrete and finite. Ships leave London daily for antipodean ports; nothing easier, if we have the means, than to buy a ticket and hire a cab to take us down to Tilbury. But this is not the end of the matter. The spirit is the thing. We must have the sharpest sense of excursion into the unknown; into a region, that is, which is not habitually our own. It is necessary, above all, to take nothing for granted. The wise traveller is he who is perpetually surprised. The stay-at-home knows that peacocks fly wild in India as starlings in England, and sees nothing to exclaim at in the fact. But the truth is, that it is a very astounding thing indeed to watch wild peacocks spread their tails in the light of an eastern sunset. Nature, with a fine rightness, planned her animals against the background of their own landscapes; it is we who have taken them away and put them in the wrong place.

So, if we are not to be surprised, or pleased with a deep, right pleasure, or are not prepared to endure an exciting but essential loneliness, we had best remain by the gas fire, looking forward to the presence of our friends at dinner. But, for my part, I would not forgo the memory of an Egyptian dawn, and the flight of herons across the morning moon.

I

IN the preface to *Eothen*, Kinglake says: "I believe I may truly
acknowledge that from all details of geographical discovery or
antiquarian research, – from all display of sound learning and
religious knowledge, – from all historical and scientific illustrations, – from all useful statistics, – from all political disqui-
sitions, – and from all good moral reflections, the volume is
thoroughly free." It reads like the Litany: Good Lord, deliver us.
Kinglake said this for his volume; I hope I shall be able to say as
much for mine. He goes on to defend the egotism of the traveller:
"His very selfishness, – his habit of referring the whole external
world to his own sensations, compels him, as it were, in the
writings, to observe the laws of perspective, – he tells you of
objects, not as he knows them to be, but as they seemed to him," –
a very reassuring passage to come upon in the writings of so
creditable an authority. Yet, when I come to think of it, why,
really, should I cite Kinglake or anybody else instead of stating the
opinion boldly as my own? We are a great deal too ready to revere
a man because he died before we ourselves saw the light. Just as I
had finished copying the passages from Kinglake, and still pleased
as I was with its appositeness, one of my favourite authors (one
who bangs the language about and makes it perform every antic
with an air of ease) came to put me sharply in my place. "Didactic
and polemical writers", he said, as I read him, propped open with
a fork on the dinner-table, "quote passages from others to support
themselves or to provide themselves with something to
controvert. . . . A writer expresses himself in words that have been
used before because they give his meaning better than he can give
it himself, or because they are beautiful or witty, or because he
expects them to touch a chord of association in the reader, or
because he wishes to show that he is learned or well-read. Quotations due to the last motive are invariably ill-advised; the dis-
cerning reader detects it, and is contemptuous; the undiscerning is
perhaps impressed, but even then is at the same time repelled,
pretentious quotations being the surest road to tedium; the less
experienced a writer is, and therefore on the whole the less well-
read he is also, the more is he tempted to this error; the experienced
knows he had better avoid it; and the well-read, aware that he
could quote if he would, is not afraid that readers will think he
cannot." That was enough to make me examine my conscience
pretty severely; and having done so, to discover for which of those

many reasons I had dragged Kinglake in, I came to the conclusion that I had dragged him in simply because he had given my meaning better than I could hope to give it myself. Learned I am not; well-read only in scraps; polemical not at all; didactic: I hope not, but am not very sure. Anyway, intimidated I would not be, so I let the Kinglake stand. He said what I meant. What more odious than the informative book of travel? unless, indeed, it sets out to be frankly so, in which case it enters into a different category, and must become, in the language of reviewers, 'monumental', 'scholarly', 'a fine tribute to the history and genius of the ... nation'. If not that, then by all means let it be frankly personal, reflecting the weaknesses, the predilections, even the sentimentalities, of the writer; let him be unashamed; let him write to his public as to a familiar friend. The art of writing, however, is a peculiar one, labouring under this disadvantage, that the arbiter is the public, uninitiated to the formulæ of the literary creed, and judging literary work by the public's own standard: the purely human, workaday standard; "good, oh, of course, *good*, but too depressing", we hear of some novel that has not provided the happy ending, all judgement of skill, or surprising, personal angle of vision, left out; which leads one to believe that nothing but an escape from workaday life is demanded from literature; that literature, in fact, is to-day but a pleasant survival, a means of escape into a world of soothing, romantic unreality; rather like looking at suits of armour in the Victoria and Albert Museum.

This, alas, is not the function of literature as those who love letters and the English tongue conceive it. For them, there is an art which depends not merely on the agreeable or the disagreeable, the disquieting, – and although this age is disquieting in the extreme, there is no reason why an opiate should be found in literature rather than elsewhere, – a perennial art, which (although in itself probably as fallacious as all other arts) must hold its own, independent of the uncomfortable everyday disquiet of the age in which it exists. But all this is irrelevant; this book is not fiction, and as for the happy ending it is obvious that the author (who may stand for hero, heroine, and all the other characters as well) cannot meet with a tragic death in the closing pages, or the book would never have been written at all.

One January morning, then, I set out; not on a very adventurous journey, perhaps, but on one that should take me to an unexploited country whose very name, printed on my luggage labels, seemed to distil a faint, far aroma in the chill air of Victoria Station: PERSIA. It was quite unnecessary for me to have had those labels printed. They did not help the railway authorities or the porters in the least. But I enjoyed seeing my fellow-passengers squint at the address, fellow-passengers whose destination was Mürren or Cannes, and if I put my bag in the rack myself I always managed to let the label dangle, a little orange flag of ostentation. How subtle is the relationship between the traveller and his luggage! He knows, as no one else knows, its idiosyncrasies, its contents; he may have for it a feeling of tenderness or a great loathing; but, for better or worse, he is bound to it; its loss is his despair; to recover it he will forego railway tickets and steamship berths; it is still with him even when he has locked himself away in the drab bedroom of a strange hotel. There is the friendly box, which contains his immediate requisites, and which is opened and shut a dozen times a day; there are the boxes which will not shut, and which therefore he takes care never to open, however badly he may need an object lurking in their depths; to unpack them altogether is unthinkable, as bad as trying to put the djinn back into the bottle. There are the miscellaneous bits – a hold-all with rugs and coats; and always some small nuisance which he wishes he had not brought; had known, indeed, before starting that he would regret it, but brought it all the same. With what a distinction, too, are invested those of his possessions which have been chosen to accompany him; he knows that he has left behind him an untidy room, with open drawers and ransacked cupboards, the floor strewn with bits of tissue paper and string; a room abandoned for somebody else to tidy up, while *he* sits smug in his carriage, having got away and escaped; and with him go, stowed away in the dark rectangular jumble of pigskin, fibre, or alligator, those patient, faithful indispensables which will see the light again in bewilderingly changed surroundings, but which for him will emerge always with the association of his own dressing-table, his own washstand, and all the close familiarity of home. They have shared his ordinary life; now they are sharing his truancy; when he and they get home again, they will look at one another with the glance of complicity.

There is a great art in knowing what to take. The box which is to be opened and shut a dozen times a day *must* be an expanding box, and to start with it must be packed at its minimum, not its maximum, capacity. This is the first rule, and all temptations to break it by last-minute cramming must be resisted. A cushion or a pillow is a bulky bother, but well worth it for comfort; an air-cushion is less of a bother, but also less of a comfort. A Jaeger sleeping-bag (which goes in the hold-all) makes the whole difference to life on a long and varied journey; but it ought to be lined with a second bag made out of a sheet, or else it tickles. I had neglected this precaution. Thermos bottles are overrated; they either break or leak or both; and there are few places where you cannot get tea. Other essentials are a knife and a corkscrew, and a hat which will not blow off. An implement for picking stones out of horses' hooves is not necessary. Quinine for hot countries, iodine, aspirin, chlorodyne, sticking-plaster. I would say: avoid all registered luggage, but there are few who will follow this sound advice. I did not follow it myself. I had a green cabin trunk, which I grew to hate, and left behind in Persia. I had, however, the excuse that I must provide against a variety of climates; I expected to be now boiled, now frozen; must have a fur cap and a sun-helmet, a fur coat and silk garments. My belongings had looked very incongruous when they lay scattered about my room.

Equipped, then, and as self-contained as the snail, the English traveller makes the most of the two hours between London and Dover. He looks out over the fields which, on the other side of the Channel, will widen out into the hedgeless sweeps of Northern France. For my part I know that line all too well; it takes me through my own fields, past my own station, and a curious mixture stirs in me; there is a dragging at the heart, and then to correct it I think deliberately how often I have seen this very train hurtle through the station, and have had a different dragging at the heart as 'Continental Boat Express' whisked past me – a wish to be off, an envy of those people sitting at the Pullman windows; but no, that was not a dragging at the heart, but at the spirit; it is home which drags the heart; it is the spirit which is beckoned by the unknown. The heart wants to stay in the familiar safety; the spirit, pricking, wants to explore, to leap off the cliffs. All the landmarks flash past me: there are the two factory pistons which go up and down, near Orpington, plunging up and down alternately, but never quite together; that is to say, one of them is not quite risen before the other has begun to fall; ever since I was a child those pistons have distressed me, because I could not get them to work in unison, side by side as they are. I know that I shall remember them, travelling across Asia; and that on my return I shall see them again, still going up and down, and still a little wrong. Then comes my own station, and Yew Tree Cottage, and the path across the fields. But would I, if I could, get out of the train and run home by that path across the fields? There is the orange label dangling: PERSIA. In half an hour I should be home; and my spaniel, sitting on my glove, would run out astonished; but meanwhile the train has rushed me into less poignant country; I am carried beyond that little patch of acres, beyond the woods where the orchis grows. I wonder whether the things in my luggage have felt a similar pull? responded, as the needle of the compass to the north?

Everything begins to recede: home, friends; a pleasant feeling of superiority mops up, like a sponge, the trailing melancholy of departure. An effort of will; and in a twinkling I have thought myself over into the other mood, the dangerous mood, the mood of going-out. How exhilarating it is, to be thus self-contained; to depend for happiness on no material comfort; to be rid of such sentimentality as attaches to the dear familiar; to be open, vulnerable, receptive! If there is a pain growling somewhere in me, I shall ignore it. Life is too rich for us to stick doggedly to the one humour.

France is familiar still, and too thickly crowded with cheap associations to be really satisfactory. Italy, under a white blanket of snow, wears an odd contrary look; for I have never seen this Lombard plain in winter, but remember it always in spring or autumn, either fresh with Star-of-Bethlehem and grape hyacinths (so sweet scented here, as they never are in England), or burnished with maize and vines. The very names of stations have a warm, autumnal smell about them: Brescia, Verona; and I remember how once I woke in Verona to hear midnight striking, and lay awake, overcome by the Shakespearean romance of it, quite sufficient already; but then, five minutes later, heard midnight strike again, on a different, dissentient clock; two Veronese midnights, where one alone had sufficed to fill me with delight! This obvious, silly thing humbled me with gratitude, as a beggar that has been suddenly enriched with royal alms. I savoured the special pleasure of travelling over ground already sharpened by a previous experience; of dwelling with a sensuous slowness on old, revived memories; when the future is full of the promise of new experience, pregnant with a prophetic sense of memory, as though the spirit had rushed forward and had come back, bringing with it hints of treasure, as the spies brought fruits from the promised land.

Then at Trieste I stepped off the edge of Europe; saw portions of Europe still, from deck: the coast of Greece at dawn, the coast of Crete at sunset, a rainbow standing marvellously on end on the bare cliffs; but knew that I should set no foot on Europe till I returned again out of Asia. Meanwhile the ship, being top-heavy, rolled as though she meant to turn turtle; passengers drifted away, and reappeared no more; very few remained to eat or even to admire the food devised by the playful Italian fancy: polar-bears made of sugar stalking one another round a rock of ice internally illuminated by electric light; glass and crockery rushed from one side of the ship to the other as she rolled, no provision apparently having been made for their restraint; but on the fourth morning we woke in summer, the rough January seas left behind, and presently on the horizon appeared the low coast of Africa.

II

Earlier memories of Cairo were scarcely agreeable; very young, very shy, and very awkward, I had been made to stay with Kitchener. I had not wanted to stay with him; I had protested loudly; my relations, who thought they knew better, said that some day I should be glad to have gone. I was not then, and am not yet, glad; for the recollection survives with horror, a sort of scar on the mind. I had arrived at the Residency suffering from a sunstroke and complete loss of voice – not an ideal condition in which to

Sunset on the Nile at Luxor.

confront that formidable soldier. Craving only for bed and a dark room, I had gone down to dinner. Six or eight speechless, intimidated officers sat round the table; Kitchener's bleary eye roamed over them; my own hoarse whisper alone punctuated the silence. Egyptian art came up as a topic. "I can't", growled Kitchener, "think much of a people who drew cats the same for four thousand years." I could think of nothing more to say, even had I been physically capable of saying it. Worse followed; for as we sat on the terrace after dinner, looking across the garden towards the Nile, a quick, happy patter came across the bare floor and in trotted an alert yellow mongrel. "Good gracious, what's that? a *dog*?" cried Kitchener, glaring at his A.D.C. The sanctity of the Residency was outraged; a dozen swords were ready to leap from their scabbards. I could not sit by and see murder done; I had to own that the dog was mine.

Next day, however, my host took me to the Zoo, as pleased as a child with the baby elephant which had been taught to salute him with its trunk. The ice was broken.

This time, after the lapse of years, I was irresponsibly in Egypt again; no dog to conceal, no servants, no Kitchener, no sunstroke. I went to Luxor. I had nine days' grace between ship and ship. Blankets of magenta bougainvillea hung over the white walls of Luxor; four creamy Nubian camels knelt beside the Nile. I remembered how on that previous occasion in Luxor I had lain in a cool dark room, sick with headache, but thankful to have escaped and to have my sunstroke at last to myself. Instead of going to the Valley of the Kings I had lain watching the bars of sunlight between the slats of the Venetian blinds, and hearing, with the peculiar vividness that only the concentrated egoism of illness brings, the drops of water falling on the tiled floor outside, as the servant

The Valley of the Kings at Luxor. Howard Carter was excavating the tomb of Tutenkhamun and Vita wrote to Virginia Woolf, "Two days ago they found two more chambers full of things", but unaccountably fails to mention them in her text.

splashed it from a bucket; a pleasant way of spending the days, – and even the pain seemed to add something, to mark off that week from ordinary life, – I was not resentful, only a little wistful at having to come as far as Luxor in order to do it. Now all was changed, and full of energy I took the dazzling, naked road that leads to the Valley of the Kings. How far away now appeared the English fields, – yet the two pistons were still going unevenly up and down; small and very brightly green they appeared, as though seen down the wrong end of a telescope, when I thought suddenly of them in the midst of the Theban hills. But above all they presented themselves to me as extremely populous, full of small busy life, rabbits at evening coming out from the spinneys, hares sitting on their haunches among the clods of ploughed lands, field-mice, stoats, slinking through the leaves, and birds innumerable hopping in branches; a multitudinous population of tiny things, with plenty of rich corn and undergrowth to shelter them; very soft, green, and cushioned Kent appeared to me, as I paused in the white dust of that lifeless landscape. A hoopoe? a lizard? a snake? no, there was nothing; only the tumbled boulders and the glare of the sun. This silence and lifelessness frightened me. The rocks closed in on the road, threatening. There is a keen excitement in not knowing what one is going to see next; the mind, strung up, reaches forward for an image to expect, and finds nothing; it is

like picking up a jug of water which you believe to be full, and
finding it empty. I had formed no image of the burial-ground of the
Pharaohs. Indeed, it seemed incredible that within a few moments I
should behold it with my eyes, and know for the rest of my life
thereafter exactly what it looked like. Then it would seem equally
incredible that I should not always have known. These small but
stinging reflections kept me lingering; I was loth to part with my
ignorance; I reproached myself with having wasted so many years
in not speculating on this royal sepulchre. Never again would that
delight be within my reach; for the pleasures of the imagination
I was about to exchange the dreary fact of knowledge. Already I
had seen the road, and, even were I magically to be whisked back
to Luxor, or, like Habakkuk, picked up by the hair of the head
and through the vehemency of an angelic spirit set down to give
my luncheon to some one a thousand leagues distant, still I should
have seen the road and might form some idea, on a solid basis, of
what was likely to be revealed round the corner. It was no good
turning round and going back, out of this wilderness to the narrow
green reaches of the Nile: I went forward.

III

Then there were other days at Luxor; the day when I went to the
potters' village on the edge of the desert, through the fields of
young corn where the white egrets stalked and the water-wheel
complained, as it poured its little buckets into the irrigation trench.
I liked getting away from the roads, into the region of country life,
where only the peasants laboured, bending down over the dark
earth. Everything there was slow, quiet, and regular; husbandry is
of all ages and all countries. Nothing dates. There is a special
concentration in this husbandry of the valley of the Nile; everything
is drawn tightly together; there is no sprawling. The very centuries
shrink up, and the life of man with his beasts becomes very close.
They seem to have acquired the same gait and colour, through
long association with each other and with the earth. In long files,
flat as a fresco, they trail along the dykes, mud-coloured: the
camels, the buffaloes, the little donkeys, and the man. Slouching
they go, in an eternal procession; with the Egyptian genius for
design, as though they were drawn with a hard, sharp pencil on
the sky. First the camels' heads, swaying on their long necks; then
the buffaloes, slouching as though they had just dragged themselves
out of the primeval slime; then the donkeys, with a little boy sitting
on the last rump, drumming his heels. Then the man, small but
erect, driving the lot before him. He drives, but he is part of the
procession; he brings up the rear. He completes the pattern. Yet
he is not so very different from his beasts, only perpendicular
whereas they are horizontal; he is the same colour, though he plies
a stick. Where they are all going to Heaven knows; they all seem

to be trailing on an eternal pilgrimage. It is a relief to come upon a party of peasants at work in static attitudes, bent down over the earth, not walking on towards something else; with a camel near by, safely yoked, and turning the water-wheel from morning to night in the same trodden groove; this is a kind of triumph over the camel, which (with its outstretched neck) might be an animal designed to slouch onward, always at the same gait, always over

Dorothy Wellesley, the poet. She accompanied Vita as far as India, but never earned a single mention in the book, to her disgust.

the same desert, purpose subservient to pattern. A camel yoked is nature's design defeated, for the camel looks like a natural traveller, and not like a creature intended to walk round and round in the same circle. The wooden cogs squeal as they rub against one another, in the shadow of the tamarisk, and the little pitchers come up dripping out of the deep well, spilling half their water before it gets tipped out into the trench; a wasteful process, but one upon which the centuries have not been able to improve. There is a downright, primitive simplicity about these Egyptian methods, but it appears to be effective, for enviable crops spring from the black earth. Water is the constant preoccupation, from the anxiety about the year's Nile – a good Nile, or a bad Nile – to the more controllable problem of irrigation. So the mind of the Egyptian peasant must be filled with the noise and flow of water, as the mind of every worker is shaped by the detail and exigency of his craft; he sees the pitchers dip and spill, as though they had become a part of himself, grown into his bones; he hears the shrill whining of the cogs, that sing a peculiar tune, like an incantation, all day as the feet of the camel pad round in the groove.

The peasants raised their heads at the sight of a stranger, for the tourists stick to the tombs and temples, and do not wander in the fields. The blue shirts showed above the corn as the labourers straightened their bent backs, and paused to stare. In the villages the dogs rushed out to bark, and hordes of children appeared from nowhere, with little grinning faces and outstretched palms, and bare feet scuffling in the dust. These people live in conditions of unbelievable simplicity. Their houses are mere shelters of sun-dried mud, without any furniture of even the roughest description; there

The oasis at Amari where Vita found the potters.

are simply four walls and a trodden floor; that is all. Sometimes a rude door keeps the entrance from the village street, but more often the entrance is just a hole in the wall, and anybody can look in. The potters' village was largely built of broken pots, embedded in mud; under a roof of plaited reeds, two potters sat at their work, the wheel spinning beneath the kick of their foot, their arms plunged up to the elbow in the dark wet clay, which in a minute was transformed from a shapeless lump into a jar of plain but faultless line – a precision of workmanship which contrasted oddly with the almost bestial condition of their dwellings. These are the people who can do one thing, and will continue to do it all their lives, as their ancestors did it before them, through the burning summers when no tourist dreams of going to Luxor, as through the more merciful winter when foreigners with the whole complexity of civilisation seething in their brains come to intercept for a brief moment this different current of human existence. The potters scarcely troubled to look up, they gave one dull, indifferent glance,

The potters of Amari "raised their heads at the sight of a stranger".

then flung another slab of clay on the twirling wheel, and spun it out into the slender throat of the pitcher.

A patient people. I had watched them working at some excavations, a long stream of them, ascending and descending like the angels on Jacob's ladder, carrying little baskets of sand and rubbish on their heads. So must the children of Israel have laboured under the lash of the taskmaster, for even now in the twentieth century the taskmasters stood by, curling their knotted thongs round the ragged limbs of the laggards. Nothing could have given so poignantly the sense of the cheapness and abundance of labour as the size of the little baskets; not much bigger than a punnet of strawberries, they were scarcely a load for a child, yet young men and women fetched them from out of the deep tomb, carried them up, and emptied them on the growing heap where the sun glared on the rocks. As they climbed and descended, they chanted a monotonous song; when the lash fell on them, they skipped into the air, but very good-humouredly, as though the lash were all in the day's work and fell with impartiality, more to keep the ranks on the move than to chastise the individual; so they gradually emptied the tomb which their forefathers had dug, and which time had silted up until the day should come for the curious foreigner to expose again the underground chambers, the rigid images of god and Pharaoh; only when the sunset whistle suddenly blew did they turn from beasts of burden into human beings, breaking their ranks and scattering like a flock of starlings at the clapping of hands. Then they ran and leapt over the rocks, some going away to ease themselves, others to drink thirstily from pannikins, but all joyful at their release, and childish in their demonstrations of pleasure. Blue rags and brown rags, white teeth and sinewy shanks, they must have looked very much the same when they honeycombed the Valley of the Kings, under the peaked hill, tunnelling a city underground, with passages and chambers, for the extraordinary apparatus of royal death. Nor had they themselves, among their plebeian number, been without honour, for a Pharaoh gave his gardener a tomb, and painted the roof and walls with leaves, grapes, and peaches; so that going from the royal catacombs, with their conventionalised, meaningless frescoes, into that small sepulchre overhung with fruits, was like passing from an empty palace into a living arbour. The symbols of fertility of Amon-Ra were gross and unconvincing beside the touching evidence of the gardener's toil and his master's gratitude.

The potters had pigeons for neighbours in the next village. It was a village, not of houses, but of round dove-cotes. The inhabitants arrived and departed by air, entering and leaving not by doors, but by little arched holes twenty feet above ground, and the whole place was full of the swish of wings and amorous conversation. I wondered whether they had evolved any form of self-government, like ants and bees, but they certainly seemed to be bent on nothing but courtship, preening and prinking round one another there in the Egyptian dust exactly like pigeons on a barn roof in Sussex. It was no pretty fancy, but practical observation, that gave the pigeons to Aphrodite; and these Egyptian swains were as true as the Greek to their reputation. It was a regular little town that man had built for them, with a street down the middle, and a palm-grove, and a sort of square where they might hold their civic meetings, and then those tall, round towers, honeycombed with entrances, and little ledges to sit on in the stillness of the evening.

I was reminded of all the stories in which an entire population is metamorphosed by magic into some kind of animal; and I felt that, could I but pronounce the necessary words, the whole of this gentle community would at once be restored to their rightful forms.

IV

The moon happened to be at the full while I was at Luxor, so I went out to Karnak one night after dinner, to the quick trot of two little horses. This was a thing that many people had done many times before; but to me it was egotistically invested with a special excitement; for among the ambitions that smouldered vaguely at the back of my mind, one was to see Karnak by moonlight, another was to row about Karnak in a boat; and now the first ambition was to be fulfilled. At first the horses trotted softly along the sandy track, between the trees, the clicking of their hooves forming a busy, brisk little rhythm; then the landscape began to resolve itself into its characteristic properties: an obelisk appeared, then the square portico of a lesser temple on the left, then a broken avenue of squat shapes, toad-like among the shadows, then finally the mass of Karnak itself in an open space

Karnak, the name given to the northern half of the ruins at Thebes on the east bank of the Nile.

suddenly spreading out beyond the narrow road and the trees. A strange plain country, Egypt! so true to type, so expected, so platitudinous – yet so grandly transcending all these things, making sophistication appear so trivial, putting to shame all pedantry with that perennial simplicity recognised by sophisticated and primitive minds alike. There is no escape. Fastidiousness must split the hair down to its narrowest filament; but, tired, returns again to the simplest forms for an ultimate satisfaction. We come back, always, to those odd, false, true relationships, which stir our emotions in response to our finer, not our more educated, judgement: such relationships as that of a pagan temple under the moon – though why the moon should have any bearing on the temple we do not know, except that both are old, so old that both have become unreal to us; unreal, and charged with a significance we are quite at a loss reasonably to interpret, only we know obscurely that it is there; obscurely, unscientifically, and in ignorance; perhaps mistakenly, but anyway with an inward, intuitive certainty; the conjunction stirs us as an æsthetic harmony stirs us: and who shall explain such mysteries as conjunction and rhythm, intuitively felt, but not by our present crude terminology to be defined? Who shall explain, either, the bearing of visual experience upon physical experience? That which we apprehend through the eyes can surely

Part of the immense Hall of Columns in the Temple of Amen, Karnak, the greatest of all Egyptian temples, which Vita explored by moonlight.

Karnak, "that rose out of the rock and sand, with its columns like gigantic palm-trees and its capitals like spreading lotus".

have no bearing on that which we experience through the spirit? But all these words are so vague: 'spiritually', 'emotionally', 'intellectually', what does all that really mean? We fumble, knowing that somewhere round the corner lies the last, satisfying co-ordination. Meanwhile, certain queer comings together, such as are made by rhythm, or by pattern, or by lights and shadows, do produce a natural harmony: a harmony suggesting that the part does probably fit, somewhere, into the whole.

Leaning against Karnak, I thought: what was a work of art if not the deliberate attempt to produce, artifically, such a harmony, which in nature emerges only by accident, and with the help of such adventitious advantages as Karnak itself now enjoyed, as, the moon casting shadows, and familiar constellations wryly tilted overhead. So, architecture was not and could never be a pure art, depending as it must on natural, accidental things. But there was no denying that architecture and nature made an astounding pair of allies. I had often puzzled over the architect's platitude, that the æsthetic value of a building was independent of its site, as a picture was independent of its frame, and now understood it less than ever. This Karnak, that rose out of rock and sand, with its columns like gigantic palm-trees and its capitals like spreading lotus, gave the violent lie to such a theory. It sprawled like a magnificent monster on Egypt, enhanced by all that Egypt could give. An obelisk, rising out of the desert, gained something surely by its spiky contrast with the broad rolling waste; I floundered ignorantly, arrogantly but still apologetically, among problems I did not understand. It seemed to me that, since I had embarked on this journey, I had shed everything but the primitive pleasures of sensation. I knew myself, theoretically, to be a reasonably educated person, ready to produce theories on several subjects; yet when I called on theory now, it behaved like an ill-trained dog that will not come to the whistle, snuffing rather at new, delicious scents in the hedgerow, flushing a bird, jumping after it into the air, and landing on all fours again with a mouthful of tail-feathers. Like Kinglake's traveller, I was fit only to report of objects, not as I knew them to be, but as they seemed to me – and to read into them, I might add, a great many attributes they could not really possess.

Walking into Karnak was like walking into one of Piranesi's Prisons, solidified suddenly into stone, and grown to natural, nay, to heroic size. Piled on fantastic ruin, obelisks pricked the sky; the colossal aisle soared, its base plunged in the deepest shadow, its head lifted to the moon; shafts of light struck the columns, lay in silver druggets across the floor. The black, enormous temple was shot through and through by those broad beams of light. Beyond the aisle, a vast space littered with fallen masonry lay open to the sky. Cavernous openings, porticos, colonnades, blocks of masonry; obelisks, statues of Pharaohs, some upright, some prone; and beyond them, beyond this magnificent desolation, shrilled the thin piping of the frogs. At every point of the compass, turn which way one might, this temple, this etching by a mad genius, offered some new aspect, now beautiful, now terrible; some massing of shadow, some lofty soaring into light. It crushed the mind, since it was not the human mind that had conceived it as it now appeared, but such inhuman factors as time upon earth; and, in the sky, the mechanism of astronomy which brought the moon once more to that path overhead. But, out of the awful shadows, came suddenly a human voice, insistent, clamant for recognition. "I am a twin," it said.

I turned, and beheld a figure in noble draperies standing beside me in a patch of light. It was my dragoman, a young Bedouin of proud and handsome appearance. He was in a state of extra-ordinary excitement, as though he could not contain his news, but must, under compulsion, communicate it to somebody. "I am two months older than my brother," he said, his eyes burning with pride. "My mother kept my brother two months longer than she kept me. My father gave me *two* nurses," he said, expressively rounding his hands over his breast, "two nurses, for pleasure that I came so soon. My father never looks at my brother, he looks only at me. When my father dies, I shall be the headman of our village. I get three crops a year." He broke off, and bounded nimbly up a sort of Giant's Causeway of fallen stone; paused there, tall in his flowing robes against the sky. "Listen!" he cried, and rapped on a prostrate monolith. It gave out a note like twanged steel. He laughed with delight, as though this performance on the part of the quarried granite were one with his own excitement and his simple vanity.

CHAPTER III

TO IRAQ

I

OUR return from Luxor to Cairo must have looked like a triumphal progress through the night, seen from the desert by any stray Bedouin, for the dining-car caught fire and trailed after us like the tail of a comet down the line. The train was stopped once, certainly, and some half-hearted efforts were made to put the fire out, but these being unavailing, we started off again and hoped for the best. My handsome dragoman was terribly frightened; he forgot about being a twin, he forgot about his prowess as a hunter, and insisted that the carriage would soon "be lying down on her side". Besides, he added, robbers were in the habit of putting boulders across the line, to stop the train and plunder such passengers as might survive the accident. Our particular engine-driver was a devil, it appeared, and would charge any obstacle rather than run the risk of being thought in league with the robbers. I had seen the engine-driver, a little black man with a red handkerchief knotted round his head; he had come along from his engine to watch while the railway men tried to extinguish the dining-car, most contemptuous, with a cigarette dangling from his lips; the flames lit up his dark greasy face, and he had replied scornfully to any anxious enquiries. Finally I persuaded Nasr to go back to his own compartment, which he did, remarking that he would rather break in a rogue camel than go in a train again. As nothing happened, however, and as we arrived safely in Cairo next morning, he forgot his fears and implored me to take him on to Persia. He had seen France, England, Spain, and Italy; he had told his father he would not marry until he had seen all the world; would I not, therefore, take him to Asia that he might the more speedily settle down with a wife? He looked crestfallen when I said it was impossible, but soon brightened again. If I would not do that, would I at least send him a packet of post cards (coloured) of Shakespeare's house at Stratford? This I was able to promise, and he ran along beside the train as it moved out of Cairo station, explaining that he had left eighteenpence with the post-card shop at Stratford, but that they had never sent the post cards ... but here we reached the end of the platform, and the last I saw of him was the flutter of his white robe as he stood waving and looking after the train which might have carried him on the way to the coveted places.

He was a great dandy, and I missed him. His luggage had been a mystery to me, for he apparently carried a roll of blanket only,

yet every day in Luxor he had produced new, voluminous clothes, green, purple, and white, and scarves embroidered with gold thread, and leather shoes in purple and yellow. I wished I had his receipt. My own baggage by now had increased considerably, and my supply of orange labels was giving out; I had acquired a gramophone, an ice-box, and a large canvas bag which took the overflow of my books. The gramophone and the ice-box I had accepted in Cairo to save them from being thrown into the Nile; as they had already travelled with forty-seven other pieces of luggage over Tibet on the backs of yaks, I thought it a pity they should not continue their career.

With this paraphernalia I arrived at Port Said; learnt that the ship was late; slept in an hotel on the quay-side; and woke in the morning to find the liner moored under my windows.

II

In due course we came to Aden, which of all outposts of empire seemed to me the most forlorn and disagreeable, though an old soldier on board told me it was "not so bad, – you get cheap polo, and shoot lion in Somaliland". I hope this proves a compensation to the unfortunate regiments stationed there; for my part, I would as soon throw myself to the sharks as live in that arid, salty hell. That Rimbaud should have endured it, should have endured the Hôtel de l'Univers, is a real tribute to the horrors of Aden; for it was to be expected that Rimbaud, with that perversity which made him renounce literature at the age of nineteen, should inflict upon himself a sojourn in precisely the most repulsive corner of the world he could find. Nevertheless, that day at Aden had a certain style of its own, if style is to be held to depend upon judicious exaggeration; it was grotesque, it was nightmareish. Some Parsee friends I had made on the boat induced me to land; we were taken off in a motor-launch by a very old and distinguished Parsee merchant in a shiny black hat, who placed his secretary, a dark scornful young man in white ducks, and his motor at our disposal for the rest of the day. In this ramshackle machine we were driven at furious rate, and in a howling gale, over the whole of that unpleasant region. First up to the chain of tanks, vast cement pits of unknown antiquity and Dantesque fearfulness, situated where a narrow gorge descended from the hills; designed to hold water, in a district where no rivers run and rain falls once in ten years, one of them – the largest – did display a green, stagnant puddle at the bottom, but otherwise the bone-dry nakedness of their concrete slopes resembled nothing so much as the Mappin terraces at the Zoo, inhabited not by bears, but by two small, nude, black boys, who beat with their fists on their stomachs, producing a curious reverberation, and cried incessantly, "No fader, no moder, thank-you", to the party of strangers peering over the top. Incongruous

Vita Sackville-West on board S.S. *Rajputana* on which she sailed from Port Said to Bombay.

figures in the scene were some Scotch soldiers, gazing wistfully at the tanks which they must have seen a hundred times before; kilts at Aden! We are too well accustomed to the kilt, but present it to the foreign eye and observe the effect; is it not Mme. de Noailles who speaks so appreciatively of the *"miroitement des genoux roses"*? We left the Scotch soldiers, who transferred their wistful gaze to us, fortunate birds of passage while they must remain behind, re-entered the motor, and were driven away at the same furious rate, into the bowels of the earth this time, with screaming siren down a long tunnel, scattering camels and shaven Somalis as we went, only to emerge on a landscape more hideous than any we had yet seen. It was perfectly flat and desolate, blanched by great patches of salt. There are few manifestations of nature which are wholly ugly, but salt is one of them. It spreads over the ground like a sort of leprosy, till 'salt of the earth' seems dubious praise. Quite in vain we protested that we did not want to see the salt-fields; the scornful young secretary was determined, and, lolling beside the chauffeur, urged him along the road with a flick of the hand, while we in the back clung to our hats and tried at the same time to safeguard ourselves against being jolted out of the motor. After what seemed miles of travelling we reached the salt-fields; the air was bitter with brine, great heaps of white salt stood like rows of tents, disused windmills spread their motionless sails. The secretary invited us to admire; we were thankful for the breathing space; we shook out our clothes and tried to rub some of the dust out of our eyes. Now, surely, we might be allowed to return to Aden. Not at all, there was a garden we must visit. Remorselessly we were hurled towards the garden, through a Somali village; flew through the garden, in at one gate and out of the other, then back towards Aden, dashing round corners, tearing down hills, all the while with the hot wind howling across the sand and raising clouds of grit that lashed our faces. Mazeppa himself had not a more

The salt-fields of Aden where "disused windmills spread their motionless sails".

horrific ride. The secretary alone seemed pleased. We arrived at the town, and were already beginning to think of the peaceful cabins of our anchored ship, when the car stopped with a jerk outside a Ford garage, and we were invited to alight. Too dazed by now to offer resistance, we followed the secretary into the yard, where stood a quantity of scrap-iron and broken-down lorries. Was this one of the sights of Aden? "Lions," observed the secretary with pride, and there indeed among the lorries and lumber were two mangy lions in an exceedingly small cage. We looked dutifully at these two poor animals, who stared past us after the manner of their kind in the direction of their native Africa; the secretary lolled by the cage, a supercilious smile on his lips. We were not yet to escape him, for he then took us firmly to his master's house. After the tanks, the tunnel, the wind, the salt, and the lions, this was an agreeable place, and one that might have done for the setting of a Conrad novel. A low, dark, aromatic, apothecary's shop on the ground floor; high, airy rooms upstairs, with marble floors, models of ships in glass vases, bunches of herbs hung in festoons across the lintels of the doors, ledgers scattered upon the tables. Here, after one of those uncomfortable waits during which, because one is in a stranger's house, one talks in a lowered voice, the old Parsee joined us. He was accompanied this time by his granddaughter, a yellow-faced child wearing on her dark black hair a round cap like a golden muffin. The secretary lolled in the doorway, sucking the top of his cane. Bare-footed Indian servants brought tea and sweet biscuits. Conversation was a little difficult; we did not like to pass any comments on Aden to this old merchant-prince, who by virtue of his wealth and importance in the town was entitled to call himself Adenvala, and who sat stirring his tea, his eyes downcast, a slight and unexplained smile wrinkling the corners of his mouth. We could only admire his photograph of the Prince of Wales, and a rather faded group taken on board the *Ophir*, while he expressed –

cynical and shrewd old trader that he was – his loyalty to the British flag.

I hope I shall never have cause to call myself Adenvala. I leant over the side of the ship that evening while the hawks and gulls circled with wild cries disputing between them the ship's refuse, and wondered whether I should ever see Aden, with its tanks and lions, or Mr. Kaikobad Cavasjee Dinshaw Adenvala again. I determined at least that I would not travel to Persia again by that route if I could help it.

III

To one ignorant of the principles of navigation it seems miraculous that after four days of steaming across apparently unidentifiable wastes of ocean the ship should hit off with such exactitude the correct but narrow harbour-bar on a distant strand. That she should, sooner or later, with the aid of the compass, hit, at some point, the coast of India seems plausible enough, but that she should slide thus unerringly between the buoys of Bombay, without having first to feel about for them, remains one of those mysteries which no amount of explanation will ever lessen. I could not believe my eyes when, waking at four o'clock one morning in an unnatural stillness, I looked out of my porthole and saw, instead of the familiar circle of waters, the dawn scarlet behind a range of hills. Small craft were dotted about; kites swept over the placid surface; yellow lights ringed the water's edge; rigging pencilled the flaming sky. Here was all the business of land again, albeit a land unawakened as yet, unmindful of the ship that stole thus clandestinely to her berth in the sleeping hours before the renewed activity of early day. So the maps had been right after all, and there was a continent on the other side of that interminable ocean! I had grown so quickly accustomed to running up on deck at dawn, and to watching the day grow over what might well have been the same ring of ocean morning after morning, that I now looked with astonishment at quays and buildings, and at the solid India that rose beyond the amphitheatre of the harbour.

IV

Curiously little remains to me of India: it seems to me now that I have never been there; only a few things stand out, but they are detached, as though I had seen them through a hole cut in a mask, with their enormous surroundings blacked out, leaving them bright and isolated. A bridge over a river, crowded with animals: horns and patient faces; a sea of animals' backs; I see the sticks of the drivers rising and falling on the grey, bristly backs of buffaloes; I see the horned heads turning, in a meek, uncomprehending wish to obey; I see the glittering river below, and the stretches of white dazzling sand; and then again the shadowy bridge, with that great,

The Taj Mahal, Agra, which she described to Virginia Woolf as "a pure and sudden lyric". It was one of the few places in India which gave her pleasure.

slowly moving concourse, as though all the herds in the world
were being driven to the final slaughter. Then I see a long road at
twilight, bordered by trees, and a jackal looking at me out of the
scrub. Then I see a red city straggling over a hill; there are shrill
green parrots there, and monkeys; and the curved brown body of
a man falling from an immense height into a green pool below. A
red city, and the genius of Akbar; a white city, and the genius of
Lutyens; the Moghul Empire, and the British. But none of this

The Viceroy's palace at
New Delhi which in 1926
was only half-built.
There Vita met its archi-
tect, Sir Edwin Lutyens,
an old family friend.

bears any relation to India; India is too vast, too diverse, to be
grasped as a whole, therefore only details emerge. I know that for
two days and nights I travelled shut up in a stifling little box with
smoked windows, which was a railway carriage but which seemed
to me like the Black Hole of Calcutta on wheels, and that through
the windows I watched the enormous areas go past, disappointingly
like an English park down in the plains, but climbing through
Bhopal into Gwalior up a track cut through the jungle, crossing
ravines and passing hills of square sugar-loaf shape; leaning out I
could look down the long serpent-like curve of the train, and see
a forest of brown legs and arms hanging out of the windows to

cool; and that was India, but almost before I knew it I was back
in Bombay harbour, on another boat, heading north for Karachi and the Persian Gulf.

V

By this time I had come to look on my journey as a series of zigzag lines, shooting across the map: a long dash south, to Aden; a long dash east, to Bombay – nearly straight, those two lines; – now there was to be added a long dash north-west to Bagdad, a line with several obtuse angles in it, and finally an easterly line, shooting like the beam of a searchlight into Asia. Long thin lines they were, no thicker than lines made with an etching pen.

I had looked forward to sailing up the Persian Gulf. There are some places whose names invest them with every kind of suggestion, and this was one of them; its name in French, too, had an odd little twist to it: *le Golfe Persique*. Why *persique*? Why not *persan*? I imagined that I should see pearl-fisheries, and the extraordinary Phœnician mounds of Bahrein; I went over all the names of ports: Muscat, Hormuz, Koweit, Bunder Abbas, Bushire. And it was one of the hottest places on the earth; so torrid, that the inhabitants said that only a sheet of paper was spread there between man and hell. It would not be hot at that time of the year, but surely the heat to come would be felt as a threat, an unescapable thing awaited in terror; the terrible summer to come, and all the past summers that had been endured? The more I thought about it, the more did it work on my imagination, till I was in a state of superstitious trepidation about the Gulf. That wedge of sea driven up between Arabia and Persia, that place of fever, pearls, and monsoons.

But, like most things to which one has looked forward, the Gulf turned out a disappointment. It was not only a disappointment, but a nightmare. For one thing, I had sprained my ankle the day before embarking at Bombay, and it is not much fun hopping up gangways, and up and down a ship's companion, on two sticks with one dangling foot. That, however, I could have borne; but before we had been twenty-four hours at sea my temperature rushed up to a hundred and four. It was very hot and damp. I lay in my tiny cabin and wished to die. A little black steward in white ducks brought me lime-juice; he was a kindly little man, and never left my cabin without turning round to make a bow and to say ceremoniously, "I am sor-ry," but to my disordered mind he was merely sinister, a figure out of a Conrad novel, with his black face and hands, and his white clothes, and his eternal glass of lime-juice with the two straws sticking out of it. He was, however, the only human being I saw for three days, except when once I crawled on deck and watched the Hindu steerage passengers throwing cocoanuts into the sea to propitiate the deity of a temple dimly visible on the skyline. This was before we came to Karachi, our port of call, where we finally turned our backs on India. For some reason I had made up my mind that I had got diphtheria, and should be landed at Karachi to die there in hospital, so it was with relief that I heard the anchor being got up at Karachi, and the engine throb again, and knew that for better or worse they must now take me on to Basrah. Such were my forlorn and absurd imaginings. The days passed somehow, in a haze of sleep and fever; I had three principal amusements: taking my temperature, which fluctuated wildly; gargling; and examining my ankle, with a certain snobbish regret that I had no one to exhibit it to, for by now it had developed all the colours of a stormy sunset. At the end of four days I decided that I was tired of being ill; smashed my thermometer; dressed; and then, weak, thin, and hot, limped up on deck. The little ship was steaming along on a grey, placid sea. The pink cliffs of Baluchistan stretched along the horizon. I fetched a deck-chair, pen, and paper, and began this book.

VI

Fever sharpens the wits and improves the perceptions; loneliness performs the same good office. I had no one to talk to, except the captain, a jovial Scotchman who accepted his fate with the usual philosophy of such men. Yes, he said, it could be quite warm enough in the Gulf, certainly; and yes, the monsoons did give you a bit of a dusting. "But it's surprising", he added, 'what a hammering a ship will take from the sea and come up smiling." A seafaring life begets, not a lyrical, but a matter-of-fact point of view; there is, mentally, a family likeness among sailors, and this captain reminded me of another one who, on returning a borrowed copy of *Typhoon*, remarked only, "Seems to have been a bit of dirty weather knocking about." The captain, however, had to go back to his bridge and I was left to my own devices. There was not much to look at: Baluchistan was very faint, more like a long, low, pink cloud than solid land, nor had we any prospect of future sights, for the captain told me that we should pass through the narrow Gulf of Oman during the night. Ships seem to take a pleasure in passing during the dark hours any object which might be of interest to their passengers. So my hand flew over the paper, covering sheet after sheet, and a school of porpoises followed the ship, turning over and over because they are still looking for Solomon's ring, which he dropped off his finger in the Persian Gulf. Presently back came the captain, and pointed to the coast. "Persia", he said laconically.

VII

The next two days were rough and cold; no land was in sight; we might have been in the North Sea instead of the Persian Gulf. The fever returned with fury. But I was so elated that I did not care: I had begun a book, and I had seen Persia. Since I might not behold the pearls of Bahrain, I took refuge in the pearls of Proust, heavy on the white throat of the duchesse de Guermantes; I dived into my canvas bag and brought out those shabby volumes which had won me such black looks when they lay scattered round me on the deck of the P. & O.; for although parson and colonel's lady had enough French and enough Biblical knowledge to understand the titles, I doubt whether they had ever heard of Proust; anyway, I fished them out again now, and lost myself in that brilliant world, so real in its unreality. To read of Proust's parties in the Persian Gulf is an experience I can recommend, as a paradox which may please the most fastidious taste. Indeed, I came to believe that every book should be read in the most incongruous surroundings

A street scene in Basrah.

The Shat-el-Arab at Mohammerah, the narrow waterway which connects the head of the Persian Gulf to Basrah.

possible, for then it imposes its own unity in a way that startles the reader when he has to emerge again into his own world; thus, when I passed from a ball at the hôtel de Guermantes into the little dining-saloon of s.s. *Varela*, Proust's world was still truer than the ship and I was puzzled to know, really, where I was.

Then we came to Mohammerah, and, with other ships, waited outside the bar till we could begin to go up the Shat-el-Arab. It was then twilight; the ships' lights came out one by one over a wide expanse of water; the smooth sky was streaked with red and orange behind the groves of palms; again it seemed miraculous that the ship should have made her landfall, but less miraculous this time, at the head of a narrow sea, than after the opal wastes of the Indian Ocean. So we waited for a little at the gateway to Iraq, with the engines stilled, in a peace like the peace of a lagoon. Slowly we moved up the river; it was dark by now, and the waterway was narrow: a low coast, thick with groves of date palms, through which we glided all night; from time to time I got up and looked through the porthole, but saw nothing beyond the thick, tall trees, that made an opaque wall along the banks, but whose fronded tops waved gently against a clear sky.

VIII

From Basrah to Bagdad the train runs straight over the desert; yellow, hideous, and as flat as the sea, the desert comes right up to the railway line, and stretches away to the circular horizon, unbroken save by a little scrub, a few leprous patches of salt, or the skeleton of a camel. Once, the monotony is interrupted by a mound: this is Ur of the Chaldees. Otherwise there is nothing. At one station a notice-board says: Change for Bablyon. But one does not see Babylon from the train. So I was glad enough to reach Bagdad at seven in the morning, to hear the shouts with which all movement is conducted in the East, and to see the goats picking their way with pastoral simplicity between the railway trucks. I had had quite enough by then of fending for myself, and wished only to forget about the Persian Gulf and Basrah as quickly as possible; Bagdad to me meant no Arabian Nights, but the much greater and more comforting romance of friends.

This was lucky, for any one who goes to Bagdad in search of romance will be disappointed. The Tigris rushes its yellow flood

The Tigris in Bagdad, which Vita reached by train from Basrah. "The round coracles ... swirling in the flood looked impossibly unseaworthy".

through the city, and the houses which line its banks share the inevitable picturesqueness of all houses lining a waterway; the round coracles, which cross the river laden with bales and donkeys,

swirling in the flood, looking impossibly unseaworthy, have a
peculiar character of their own; but for the rest Bagdad is a dusty jumble of mean buildings connected by atrocious streets, quagmires of mud in rainy weather, and in dry weather a series of pits and holes over which an English farmer might well hesitate to drive a waggon. In Bagdad, however, drivers are not so particular. Ford cars, battered, bent, with broken wind-screens and no trace of paint, bump hooting down the street, while camels, donkey,s and Arabs get out of the way, as best they can: any road, in the East, is a road for a motor. I confess that I was startled by the roads of Bagdad, especially after we had turned out of the main street and drove between high, blank walls along a track still studded with the stumps of palm trees recently felled; the mud was not dry here and we skidded and slithered, hitting a tree-stump and getting straightened on our course again, racketing along, tilting occasionally at an angle which defied all the laws of balance, and which in England would certainly have overturned the more conventionally minded motor.

Then: a door in the blank wall, a jerky stop, a creaking of hinges, a broadly smiling servant, a rush of dogs, a vista of garden path edged with carnations in pots, a little verandah and a little low house at the end of the path, an English voice – Gertrude Bell.

Gertrude Bell in her Bagdad garden. She was Director of Antiquities and political adviser to King Faisal. She died four months after Vita's visit, aged 58.

I had known her first in Constantinople, where she had arrived straight out of the desert, with all the evening dresses and cutlery and napery that she insisted on taking with her on her wanderings; and then in England; but here she was in her right place, in Iraq, in her own house, with her office in the city, and her white pony in a corner of the garden, and her Arab servants, and her English books, and her Babylonian shards on the mantelpiece, and her long thin nose, and her irrepressible vitality. I felt all my loneliness and despair lifted from me in a second. Had it been very hot in the Gulf? got fever, had I? but quinine would put that right; and a sprained ankle, – too bad! – and would I like breakfast first, or a bath? and I would like to see her museum, wouldn't I? did I know she was Director of Antiquities in Iraq? wasn't that a joke? and would I like to come to tea with the King? and yes, there were lots of letters for me. I limped after her as she led me down the path, talking all the time, now in English to me, now in Arabic to the eager servants. She had the gift of making every one feel suddenly eager; of making you feel that life was full and rich and exciting. I found myself laughing for the first time in ten days. The garden was small, but cool and friendly; her spaniel wagged not only his tail but his whole little body; the pony looked over the loose-box door and whinnied gently; a tame partridge hopped about the verandah; some native babies who were playing in a corner stopped playing to stare and grin. A tall, grey saluki came out of the house, beating his tail against the posts of the verandah; "I want one like that", I said, "to take up into Persia." I did want one, but I had reckoned without Gertrude's promptness. She rushed to the telephone, and as I poured cream over my porridge I heard her explaining – a friend of hers had arrived – must have a saluki at once – was leaving for Persia next day – a selection of salukis must be sent round that morning. Then she was back in her chair, pouring out information: the state of Iraq, the excavations at Ur, the need for a decent museum, what new books had come out? what was happening in England? The doctors had told her she ought not to go through another summer in Bagdad, but what should she do in England, eating out her heart for Iraq? Next year, perhaps ... but I couldn't say she looked ill, could I? I could, and did. She laughed and brushed that aside. Then, jumping up – for all her movements were quick and impatient – if I had finished my breakfast wouldn't I like my bath? and she must go to her office, but would be back for luncheon. Oh yes, and there were people to luncheon; and so, still talking, still laughing, she pinned on a hat without looking in the glass, and took her departure.

I had my bath – her house was extremely simple, and the bath just a tin saucer on the floor – and then the salukis began to arrive. They slouched in, led on strings by Arabs in white woollen robes, sheepishly smiling. Left in command, I was somewhat taken aback, so I had them all tied up to the posts of the verandah till Gertrude should return, an army of desert dogs, yellow, white, grey, elegant, but black with fleas and lumpy with ticks. I dared not go near them, but they curled up contentedly and went to sleep in the shade, and the partridge prinked round them on her dainty pink legs, investigating. At one o'clock Gertrude returned, just as my spirits were beginning to flag again, laughed heartily at this collection of dogs which her telephone message (miraculously, as it seemed to me) had called into being, shouted to the servants,

Arab women by the
Tigris in Bagdad.

ordered a bath to be prepared for the dog I should choose, unpinned
her hat, set down some pansies on her luncheon table, closed the
shutters, and gave me a rapid biography of her guests.

She was a wonderful hostess, and I felt that her personality held
together and made a centre for all those exiled Englishmen whose
other common bond was their service for Iraq. They all seemed to
be informed by the same spirit of constructive enthusiasm; but I
could not help feeling that their mission there would have been
more in the nature of drudgery than of zeal, but for the radiant
ardour of Gertrude Bell. Whatever subject she touched, she lit up;
such vitality was irresistible. We laid plans, alas, for when I should
return to Bagdad in the autumn: we would go to Babylon, we
would go to Ctesiphon, she would have got her new museum by
then. When she went back to England, if, indeed, she was compelled to go, she would write another book. . . . So we sat talking,
as friends talk who have not seen one another for a long time,
until the shadows lengthened and she said it was time to go and
see the King.

The King's house lay just outside the town; a wretched building
in a sad state of disrepair, the paving-stones of the terrace forced
up by weeds, the plaster flaking off the walls and discoloured by
large patches of damp. The King himself was a tall, dark, slim,
handsome man, looking as though he were the prey to a romantic,
an almost Byronic, melancholy; he spoke rather bad French,
addressing himself in Arabic to Gertrude when his vocabulary
failed him. They discussed what linoleum he should have in the
kitchen of his new country house. Then tea was brought in, and a
sort of pyramid of fanciful cakes, which delighted Feisal, and they
discussed at great length the merits of his new cook. Gertrude
seemed to be conversant with every detail of his housekeeping as
well as with every detail of the government of his kingdom, and
to bring as much interest to bear upon the one as upon the other.

His melancholy vanished as she twitted and chaffed him, and I watched them both – the Arab prince and the Englishwoman who were trying to build up a new Mesopotamia between them. "You see," she had said to me, "we feel here that we are trying to do something worth while, something creative and constructive"; and in spite of her deference to his royalty, in spite of the 'Sidi' that now and then she slipped into her conversation, there could be very little doubt as to which of the two was the real genius of Iraq. As we drove back into Bagdad she spoke of his loneliness; "He likes me to ring up and ask to go to tea," she said. I could readily believe it.

Her house had the peculiar property of making one feel that one was a familiar inhabitant; at the end of a day I felt already that I was part of it, like the spaniel, the pony, and the partridge (the partridge, indeed, slept in my bedroom that night, on the top of the cupboard); I suppose her life was so vivid, so vital, in every detail, that its unity could not fail to make an immediate, finished impression on the mind. But I was only a bird of passage. Next evening I left for Persia, the moon hanging full over Bagdad, and my heart warmed with the anticipation of a return to that friendly little house which now I shall never see again. The finally selected saluki sat beside me; she must be called Zurcha, said Gertrude,

Vita's saluki, Zurcha, is
given her first bath in
Gertrude Bell's house.

meaning 'yellow one'; in every street café a gramophone brayed, through the fog of smoke rising from the hubble-bubbles of the Arabs. These smoky, lighted interiors slid past me as my cab bumped towards the station; but I, clinging on to my bouncing luggage, had no leisure for their tinsel or their discord. What were Arabs to me or I to them, as we thus briefly crossed one another? they in their robes, noble and squalid, of impenetrable life; and I a traveller, making for the station? They had all the desert behind them, and I all Asia before me, Bagdad just a point of focus, a last shout of civilisation, lit by that keen spirit, that active life; and lying for me now – as though I looked down upon it from a height – between Arabia and Asia, midway between a silence and a silence.

CHAPTER IV

INTO PERSIA

I

HEAVEN knows Bagdad had seemed remote enough, at Victoria on a January morning; but now, looking towards the east, it appeared almost suburban, and the great spaces only on the point of opening out. This was the last train I should see; the last time I should be jolted with that familiar railway-clanking into the night.

A poor little train it was too, taking ten laborious hours to cover the hundred miles of its journey. It climbed from the plain into the hills, and a frosty dawn found it steaming and stationary at the railhead. Railheads are not commonly seen in Europe. In England we see them, because otherwise at certain points the train would have no choice but to run on into the sea; at Dover, at Brighton, we see them – though even at Brighton there is a branch line which goes, at a right angle, along the coast to Worthing. But in Europe we do not often see them, unless we go to Lisbon or Constantinople. Even Venice is a cheat, because the train after backing curves round again and goes merrily off through the Balkans. We are accustomed to see the rails shining away over fresh country, after we have got out and are left standing beside our luggage on the platform. But here, at Khaniquin, there was no geographical reason why the rails should leave off; why, instead of going on for a thousand, two thousand, ten thousand shining miles, they should end in a pair of blunt buffers.

Mountain air at five o'clock in the morning makes one hungry. I found the little canteen in occupation of a fellow-traveller. He was a stout man, dressed in complete riding-kit – breeches, leather gaiters, even to the hunting-crop. He recommended the porridge and we got into conversation. I said something about walking to the cars. "Walk?" he said, "I have just walked eleven thousand miles." I asked if this was the first time he had been to Persia. "*Been to Persia?*" he said, "I have been round the world seventeen times." From his accent I thought he was Scotch, but he gave me his name, told me he spoke twenty-five languages, and was a Belgian marquis. He had a secretary with him, a silent, down-trodden young man, hung with cameras, thermos bottles, and field-glasses. I never heard him speak, and I never discovered his nationality. He simply ate his breakfast as though he were not sure when he would next replenish his larder. In this he reminded me of the saluki, who, a true camp-follower, had a perfectly definite attitude towards life: eat when you can and sleep when you can, for you never know when your next meal and your next rest are coming.

There was a delay over starting, the usual delay, and meanwhile the sky turned pink behind the hills, and a long caravan of camels got up and lurched away across the plateau, their bells sounding more faintly and their extraordinary silhouettes growing blacker and more precise as they trailed out against the morning sky. Then the sun came up, the snow flushed on the distant hills, the grey morning had gone, the whole plateau was full of light. It elated me to see that the road led straight into the dawn. "The sun rises in the east," we are accustomed to say; and a new significance welled up into that empty maxim. The sun was leading the way. Indeed, to wander about the world is to become very intimately mixed up with astronomy. Familiar stars tilt, and even disappear; the Bear performs antics, Orion climbs. We become conscious of the path of the sun. At home, the heavenly phenomena pass and repass over our heads, without our troubling to lift our eyes to this display of punctual and stupendous mechanism. But the traveller notices.

Outside the station the cars were waiting, muddy, loaded, the legend TRANS-DESERT MAIL in white paint on their bonnets. They had come from Beyrout, and looked it. The marquis, smacking his gaiters with his crop, was fussing round, like the fly round the coach in the fable. Avoiding the marquis, I got the front seat in the other car, with Zurcha, who although as leggy as a colt, folded up into a surprisingly small space and immediately went to sleep. I was glad to see this, as I had not looked forward to restraining a struggling dog over five hundred miles of country, and had not been at all easy in my mind as to what a saluki

Khaniquin on the Iraq–Persian frontier, the terminus of the railway from Bagdad. Baggage was transferred to cars here for the trans-desert journey.

straight out of the desert would make of a motor. That yellow
nomad, however, accepted whatever life sent her with a perfect
and even slightly irritating philosophy. Warmth and food she
insisted on; shared my luncheon and crawled under my sheepskin,
but otherwise gave no trouble. I was relieved, but felt it a little
ungrateful of her not to notice that she was being taken into Persia.

I was myself very vividly aware of going into Persia. The nose
of the motor pointed straight at the sun; this way had come
Alexander, but not Marco Polo, not Mme. Dieulafoy, not M. de
Gobineau, not even Lord Curzon. This road, which lay between
the two wild provinces of Kurdistan and Luristan, had, until the
war, existed only as a caravan route between Persia and Bagdad;
no traveller dreamt of risking his property and possibly his life
that way. True, Nasr-ed-Din Shah had made an expedition, sum-
moning the tribal chiefs of the Kurds and Lurs to meet him,
but, being informed that among these superstitious and ignorant
brigands the Shah was commonly supposed to be a giant fifteen
feet high, and being warned that the disappointment of seeing a
man of mere ordinary stature might prove subversive to their
loyalty, yet being determined to show himself to his predatory
vassals, he hit upon an ingenious expedient. Having caused his
tent to be pitched so that the rays of the rising sun should strike
full upon it, he ordered the breast of his uniform to be sewn from
collar to hem with every diamond in the Persian treasury. The
chiefs assembled at dawn. Then, as the sun rose, the flap of the
Shah's pavilion was thrown open, and in the sun's illumination
appeared that motionless and resplendent figure. The chiefs pros-
trated themselves; but when they again raised their dazzled eyes,
the Shah had vanished.

I asked my driver if he had ever been held up on the road. No,
he said, he hadn't, but several of his mates had, because they were
fools enough to stop when ordered. "Now if anybody comes at

Strings of camels crossing the desolate country which seemed to Vita "all exactly as it
must have been when Marco Polo travelled this way".

me," he added. "I drive straight at them." With that, he let in his gears, and we started. The first few miles were atrocious, and populous. We overtook the long string of camels, and innumerable donkeys loaded with petrol tins; waggons too, with drivers asleep; lorries full of grain, some advancing, others stuck askew in the mud. Streams crossed the track every hundred yards or so, and this meant mud up to the axles; in between the streams the road was less a road full of holes, than a series of holes connected by fragments of road. Our luggage truck bounded and bounced ahead of us. There was a great deal of shouting and of digging out of stranded lorries in progress, and mingled with the shouts of the men came the grave note of the camel bells, and the creaking of the overloaded waggons. They all seemed to be going east; we met no one coming the other way. They trailed across the rolling ground towards the frontier, a straggling concourse, in the clear morning.

The Iraq frontier consisted of a post-house, a crazy gate hung across the road, and a few strands of barbed wire. Inside the post-house we were given tea and cigarettes while our passports were being stamped, and admired the collection of visiting-cards with

The Iraq frontier, five miles short of the first Persian customs post.

which the walls were papered. The marquis took a number of photographs with different kodaks. Three woolly puppies tumbled in the dust. Meanwhile the traffic accumulated into a block of waggons and animals, which we left behind us, jostling and abusive, as we swung into the No-man's land between Iraq and Persia. The Persian frontier lay about five miles ahead; here we were offered an escort of soldiers, which we declined; the pole that barred the road was raised; we moved forward; we were in Persia.

I discovered then that not one of the various intelligent people I had spoken with in England had been able to tell me anything about Persia at all – the truth being, I suppose, that different persons observe different things, and attribute to them a different degree of importance. Such a diversity of information I should not have resented; but here I was obliged to recognise that they had told me simply nothing. No one, for instance, had mentioned the beauty of the country, though they had dwelt at length, and with much exaggeration, on the discomforts of the way. It reminded me of nothing so much as the traditional reply of the negro, who, when asked, "How far is it to such-and-such a place?" replies, "Not too far." "Is the road steep?" I had asked, and had been told, "Not too steep," which was true enough of the road across the plains, but quite untrue of the road over the passes, which climbs to ten thousand feet in a seven-mile series of hairpin bends. No one had told me that I must take my own provisions for three or four days; but that, fortunately, I had found out in Bagdad. No one had told me that I might have to spend several nights in a mud hut by the roadside, held up by a fresh fall of snow, though that was constantly happening to travellers less lucky than I. No one, in fact, had made one single useful or illuminating remark. It had its advantages, and allowed me to enter Persia with an open mind. I had no idea whatever of what I was going to see.

I saw, as, with the sun, we swept onwards, a country unlike anything I had ever seen before. England, France, Germany, Poland have their points in common; a sense of care and cultivation; snug little villages; homesteads tiled and self-contained; evidences of husbandry, in ploughed fields, meadows, ricks; a trim landscape, a landscape ordered by man, and submissive to his needs. Italy and Spain have their points in common; a landscape again submissive to man, though compelling him to work on lines dictated by the rougher lie of the land: he has had to make terraces for his vines, his cities wear a rude mediæval aspect, the general wild beauty of the country has been conquered indeed, but only after a struggle; murder and pillage, Moors and tyrants, still stalk those slopes. Russia has the green rolling steppe; predominantly the face of the dry land is cultivated, it is used, it is forced to be of service to man and his creatures, it is green. But Persia had been left as it was before man's advent. Here and there he had scraped a bit of the surface, and scattered a little grain; here and there, in an oasis of poplars and fruit trees outlining a stream, he had raised a village, and his black lambs skipped under the peach-blossom; but for miles there was no sign of him, nothing but the brown plains and the blue or white mountains, and the sense of space. The crowds of Europe suddenly rushed at me, overwhelmed me; I was drowning under the pressure, when they cleared away, and I was left, breathing, with space all round me, and a serenity that looked down from the peaks on to the great bowl of the plain. The motor, as it swept up and down the hills, might have been an eagle swooping; no sooner had it reached the top of an eminence than it swept down again and was off, eating up the long road, till the smooth monotony of our movement lulled me into a sort of hypnotic state, through which I perceived the landscape rushing past; the shadows of clouds bowling over the plain as though to race the car; the occasional dark patch made by a grazing flock. We were in Kurdistan. Such peasants as we met wore long blue coats with a broad, twisted sash; high, brimless hats of felt, their black hair curling out from underneath, in the mediæval fashion; their legs were bound in rags; they carried staves and drove animals before them.

Kurdish tribesmen encountered *en route* to Teheran.

From their ragged, mediæval appearance they might have been stragglers from some routed army. They travelled on foot, on horseback, or in waggons; hooded waggons, going at a foot's pace, drawn by four little horses abreast; long strings of waggons, trailing along, heaped with rugs and household goods; a wretched, starved-looking procession. If the distances seemed great to us, sweeping along in a powerful motor, what must they have seemed to that crawling string, whose day's journey meant no change of scene, no appreciable lessening of the stretch between mountain-range and range?

We stopped to eat, that first day, by a brawling river at the foot of our first mountain-pass; then left the plain and climbed, round dizzy precipitous corners, squeezing past waggons and camels – for there is always more traffic on a pass than elsewhere: the horses cannot drag their loads, and have to be unharnessed and

reharnessed as trace-horses, and started off again, scrambling and
slipping on the stony surface. We met little donkeys, coming down,
stepping delicately, and camels, swaying down on their soft padded
feet. Looking up, we could see the whole road of the pass zigzagging
up the cliff-side, populous with animals and shouting, thrashing
men. Looking back, as we climbed, we could see the immense
prospect of the plain stretching away behind us. A savage, deso-
lating country! but one that filled me with extraordinary elation.
I had never seen anything that pleased me so well as these Persian

uplands, with their enormous views, clear light, and rocky
grandeur. This was, in detail, in actuality, the region labelled
'Persia' on the maps. Let me be aware, I said; let me savour every
mile of the way. But there were too many miles, and although I
gazed, sitting in the front seat, the warm body of the dog pressed
against me, the pungent smell of the sheepskin in my nostrils, it is
only the general horizon that I remember, and not every unfolding
of the way. This question of horizon, however; how important it
is; how it alters the shape of the mind; how it expresses, essentially,
one's ultimate sense of country! That is what can never be told in
words: the exact size, proportion, contour; the new standard to
which the mind must adjust itself.

The summit of the Peitak pass, west of Kerman-shah, where the road meets the edge of the high plateau of central Asia.

After the top of the pass I expected to drop down again, to come
down on the other side; the experience of remaining up, once one
has climbed, had not yet become familiar to me. I was not yet
accustomed to motoring along a level road, in the close company
of mountain tops. But these were the high levels of Asia. All day
we continued, until darkness fell, and the shapes of hills became

like the shapes of crouching beasts, uncertain, disquieting. This country, which all the day had been flooded with light, and which now and then had softened from its austerity into the gentler swell of hills like English downs, rounded, and bathed in light like the pink light of sunset – even at midday – now reverted to its pristine secrecy; the secrecy of days when no traveller passed that way, but only the nomad Kurds driving their flocks to other pastures; the secrecy of darker days, when the armies of Alexander and Darius, making for Ecbatana, penetrated the unmapped, tumbled region, seizing a peasant to act as guide; captain and emperor surveying from a summit the unknown distances. The moon came up from behind a hill; the full moon, whose birth I had seen netted in the rigging, in an opalescent dawn on the Indian Ocean. I watched, turning to human things, the blunt, young profile of the chauffeur under his peaked cap. I talked to him, as the air freshened and the moon climbed, and Zurcha settled closer into my arms with a contented sigh, as though I had not plucked her out of the Arabian desert, away from the life of tents and the weary sleep beside the camels' packs. He drove, his eyes on the road whitened by the stream of the headlights, and as he drove he talked, with a soft Scotch accent among the Persian hills. He was on the desert service usually, he said, Beyrout to Bagdad; that meant thirty-six hours continuous driving, with an hour's stop for dinner, rough going part of the way, no regular track, and plenty of rocks and gullies to look out for; smooth going part of the way, as smooth as a hard tennis court, and that meant seventy miles an hour for a matter of two hundred miles; this route he travelled sometimes twice a week, if drivers were short; arrived in Bagdad, he might be told to turn his car round and drive straight back. Well, he said, with a grin, we do sometimes drop asleep at the wheel. But he did not much mind, he said – one got used to it – for the pay was good, and his wife was in Beyrout. Little by little his story came out. The son of a Scotch crofter, he had gone to Russia fourteen years ago, to work on the railways; had been caught there by the war; enlisted in the Russian army; did not like it; deserted; came to England, enlisted afresh, went to France a week later, tried to return to Russia after the war, but so far had not succeeded in getting farther than Syria or Persia. He had married, but his wife went mad in Bagdad, and he had been obliged to drive her across the desert to put her into a mad-house in Beyrout. Such was the life-history which, without the air of thinking it in the least unusual, he unfolded to me. I had already heard him speak Russian and Persian with equal fluency – but our conversation was interrupted, for a wild, coloured figure on horseback came at full gallop into the glare of our headlights.

True to his word, the driver trod on the accelerator and the motor leaped at the horseman. I thought we must go straight into him, in which case he would have got the worst of it, for the car

was a heavy one, and the pony he rode was a lean, rough animal
like a Cossack pony, which must certainly have gone rolling with its rider into the ditch. Unfortunately we missed him; or, rather, with miraculous skill he swerved his pony, clearing the mud-guard by a couple of inches, and we heard the hooves go clattering down the road. The driver looked at me and grinned. "That's their trick," he said. "They come at you, and most people pull up. If I'd pulled up there would have been four or five of them round us in a minute. This is the worst part of the road." We drove on. Already, in passing through a village, a Kurd had sprung out and struck at the motor with a knobbed stick, and we had had one or two little indications of anxiety: at the toll-gates we were stopped, and escorts were offered, for telephone messages had come through from Kermanshah asking for news of our passage – it was strange to be greeted with telephone messages on that wild and lonely road; but we could not be bothered with an escort, and preferred to take our chance unhindered. I was glad we had refused those escorts, for I would not for the world have missed the brief encounter with that marauding apparition. I had felt, in seeing him, as one might feel who sees a wild animal suddenly revealed in the jungle. I was almost sorry when we saw ahead of us the lights of Kermanshah.

Kermanshah, where Harold recalls waiting for Vita "in a terrible state of impatience, anxiety and excitement". They continued together to Tehcran.

II

Next day we reached the snow. The first part of the way took us over plains again; the landscape altered a little, became more typically Persian: snow mountains in the distance, on the rim of the plain, blue and white; foothills nearer at hand, like north-country fells, tawny in the curious, intense light, tawny through every shade of brown, from yellow through ochre to burnt umber. This colour of the hills cannot be exaggerated; in variety, richness, and unexpectedness I had never seen anything to equal it. The rockier portions looked painted, artificial; patches of blue-green rock appeared, looking as though they had been sprayed with copper sulphate – copper overgrown with verdigris; rocks of pale malachite; then a ridge of blood-red rock; rocks of porphyry. The typical caravanserais began: square enclosures of dried mud, a courtyard in the middle, where the camels might spend the night; little domes of mud over the gateway. These occurred, or the ruins of them, every twenty miles or so, twenty miles being a day's march for a camel. The huts began, so-called tea-houses; mud huts, where the brass samovar boils all day, and tea may be drunk in glasses; huts which may be put to a more urgent use, as shelters, night after night, when the roads are blocked, and the traveller claims the hospitality of a mud shelf on which to spread his sheepskin, and lies there, his eyes smarting from the charcoal smoke, his drowsy gaze wandering over the group of men round the brazier, when the wind howls outside, and benighted peasants come in, stamping the snow from their shoes and rubbing their chilled fingers above the embers. As we reached the foot of the pass, and saw the road beginning to rise until it lost itself among the peaks of the summit, we could not help wondering whether we should be compelled to seek refuge in such a hut; already our ideas had begun to accommodate themselves to the emergencies of Persian travel; we had wooden shovels ominously strapped to the back of the car; we had overheard discussions as to the state of the road: a car had come through yesterday, much delayed, but between yesterday and to-day conditions might have changed; a fresh fall up there, on the top, might have blocked the road, and indeed we had met no car to-day coming in the opposite direction, from Assadabad; so we speculated, not without apprehension, but we could not linger at the foot of the pass, and started on the upward climb, the road growing steeper, the corners sharper, until the snow began, and the wheels skidded in the mud. We rose higher and higher; the snow was everywhere now, only the black, muddy road gashed it, fields of white snow, and the black road climbing in hairpin bends, littered with waggons, the flanks of the horses steaming on the air. Now the snow rose in ramparts; the road was simply a lane cut between ramparts of snow, twenty feet high, towering above the motor. Gangs of men were at work, clearing the snow; with black spectacles over their eyes, and mufflers over their mouths, they wielded their great wooden shovels; their coloured rags, and those primitive tools, whose long handles projected in black lines across the snow, gave them the aspect of the armed peasants of the French

Vita somehow managed to leave the car at intervals to photograph other travellers crossing the snowbound passes between Kermanshah and Teheran. Three thousand men, she was told, were at work to keep the passes open.

The summit of the highest pass, Assadabad, at 10 000 feet, just short of Hamadan the ancient Ecbatana.

The car convoy was accompanied on the Kasvin road by horsedrawn carts of greater elaboration than any they had encountered so far. "Wore a sheepskin coat and fur hat one day", wrote Vita to Virginia, "and a silk dress the next."

Revolution. Three thousand men, we were told, were at work, keeping the road open to let the grain lorries through, to save Teheran from famine. We crept upward, between the snow walls, and the cold increased, until we topped the summit at ten thousand feet. Here, snow lay all around us, and ahead of us lay a great white plain; only behind us, looking back over the way we had come, we looked down on to the brown plain, crossed by the ribbon of road, so that we might have been looking down on summer out of the depth of winter. Again that new sensation of staying up; for we dropped very little, and reached Hamadan to find the poplars rooted in snow, and tales of wolves current in the town.

III

This was Ecbatana, and in the path of Alexander and Darius we pursued the way. Then I remember a monotony of white plains, and another pass, – the Aveh, – less dramatic, but more unpleasant, for a bitter wind howled across it; and then the climate softened imperceptibly as we came down, and the earth appeared again, though still streaked with snow, and through groves of pistachio trees the road led us into Kasvin. Muddy, tired, and impatient, we were of course held up at the gate. These little ceremonies at the gates of cities always amused me; names must be given, papers produced, and particulars copied down with the stump of a pencil into a greasy and undecipherable notebook. Then you may go forward. This evidence of municipal care contrasts so oddly with the complete indifference to your fate once you have passed out into the country, where you may be robbed, murdered, or drowned for all that any one cares. Then on the fourth day we entered on the last lap of that journey. We were done with the snow, for which I was thankful, for the white blanket obscured the beautiful colours of the country, and hid its shapes under the soft, cotton-wool depths that were broken not even by the tracks of an animal; but here from the plain of Kasvin the foothills rose bare again, and only the tops of the Elburz and of the distant mountains were ridged with snow. The road ran perfectly straight over the plain for a hundred miles; and because it was the highway between Teheran and Kasvin, a stream of animals and vehicles flowed along it, dejected, dilapidated, with merchandise for the capital; droves of donkeys, huge caravans of camels, – which at evening turned into the caravanserais, loose, swaying heads and a forest of legs, knobbly, with great knees, all turning vaguely in the same direction, lounging in through the gateway, a forest of camels, taller than the motor, their ugly pendulous mouths swaying above us; – carts drawn by men, two in front and two behind, simply beasts of burden, who sweated and crawled onwards, not making two miles in an hour, men so low and bestial that it seemed they had not the imagination to compel an animal to serve them, but accepted their lot as slaves, plying on the Kasvin road with carts too heavy, until the strength was worn out of them. All these signs indicated that we were in the neighbourhood – as neighbourhoods go in these parts – of a town; the centre which we had travelled so many days to reach. But there were no other signs; none of those straggling outposts that begin long before the town is reached, in Europe; no detached houses, or other roads converging; only the one road, drawn like a line across the plain, with the men and beasts going along it. Vultures flapped away, rising from their horrid meal by the roadside, where a mule or a camel had fallen; thus the desert encroached, even up to the walls of the city. The city itself was not visible, though we knew we could not be more than twenty miles distant, once we had come round the elbow of the hills at Kardej, and saw Demavend before us, the smooth white mountain, the beacon, soaring into the sky. Teheran must lie there, somewhere, in the dip. To the right glimmered a golden dome, far away; the mosque of Shah Abdul Azim, said some one, and little heaps of stones appeared like mole-heaps by the road, for in Persia, where you first catch sight of your place of pilgrimage, you must raise a heap of stones to the fulfilment of your vow. I felt inclined to add my heap to the others, for it seemed to me incredible that I should at last be within walking distance of Teheran. But where *was* that city? A patch of green trees away to the left, a faint haze of blue smoke; otherwise nothing, only the open country, the mountains, the desert, and little streams in flood pouring at intervals across the road. It all seemed as forlorn and uninhabited as the loneliest stretches of Kurdistan. Yet there stood a gate, suddenly, barring the way; a gate of coloured tiles, a wide ditch, and a mud rampart, and a sentry stopping us, notebook in hand. Persian towns do surely spring upon one unawares, rising in their compact, walled circle out of the desert. But this, no doubt about it, was Teheran.

The Kasvin Gate, where Vita entered Teheran on 5 March 1926, one of twelve which in her day pierced the 12-mile circumference of the city walls. The census of 1919 gave Teheran a population of 250 000.

CHAPTER V

ROUND TEHERAN

I

THIS country through which I have been hurled for four days has become stationary at last; instead of rushing past me, it has slowed down and finally stopped; the hills stand still, they allow me to observe them; I no longer catch but a passing glimpse of them in a certain light, but may watch their changes during any hour of the day; I may walk over them and see their stones lying quiet, may become acquainted with the small life of their insects and lichens; I am no longer a traveller, but an inhabitant. I have my own house, dogs, and servants; my luggage has at last been unpacked. The ice-box is in the kitchen, the gramophone on the table, and my books are on the shelves. It is spring; long avenues of judas trees have come into flower along the roads, the valleys are full of peach-blossom, the snow is beginning to melt on the Elburz. The air, at this altitude of nearly four thousand feet, is as pure as the note of a violin. There is everywhere a sense of openness and of being at a great height; that sense of grime and over-population, never wholly absent in European countries, is wholly absent here; it is like being lifted up and set above the world on a great, wide roof – the plateau of Iran.

Teheran itself, except for the bazaars, lacks charm; it is a squalid city of bad roads, rubbish-heaps, and pariah dogs, crazy little victorias with wretched horses; a few pretentious buildings, and mean houses on the verge of collapse. But the moment you get outside the city everywhere changes. For one thing, the city remains definitely contained within its mud rampart, there are no straggling suburbs, the town is the town and the country is the country, sharply divided. For another thing, the city is so low that at a little distance it is scarcely visible; it appears as a large patch of greenery, threaded with blue smoke. I call it a city, but it is more like an enormous village. The legend here is, that a certain speculator went to the Shah and said, "King of Kings, if I build you a rampart round your city, will you give me all the land within the rampart that is not yet built over?" and the Shah, thinking the man a fool, agreed. But the man was not a fool, and he built the rampart in so wide a circle that the city has not yet grown out to its walls.

You cannot enter or leave Teheran except by a gate, which is named according to the direction of the road that leads away from it: the Meshed Gate, the Kasvin Gate, the Isfahan Gate, and so on. They are picturesque, coloured structures, faced with tiles – blue tiles, or black and yellow tiles – but dilapidated of course, like

The Isfahan Gate,
Teheran.

everything else. If you sit by the gate you will see the life of the
city streaming disconnectedly in and out of it: a string of camels,
a drove of donkeys; some pedestrians; some veiled women; a car
or two; some bicyclists – for every one in Persia rides a bicycle,
and falls off it the moment he sees another vehicle approaching. It
is quite instructive to sit by the gate for a couple of hours. You get
a very good impression of the farmyard life of eastern countries,
man so indissolubly jumbled up with his animals, especially here
in Persia (even more so, if that were possible, than in Egypt or in
India), here in Persia, where motor transport is new, and railways
nil, and where everything must be done on the back of pack
animals. The camels arrive with boxes and bales from Bagdad,
having been six or eight or ten weeks on the way; they arrive with
petrol from the south, and very odd it is to see the English words
on the crates: HIGHLY INFLAMMABLE; then the donkeys come
in, tiny grey donkeys, almost invisible, but for four poor little legs,
under an enormous load of camel-thorn for fuel; then comes a
flock of sheep, brown and black, their hard little hooves pattering
just like rain over the gravel; then a gaggle of geese, driven by a
child; then a man carrying two chickens. It is most remarkable,
the extent to which the Persians carry chickens. Why they should
walk about carrying them, in the way they do, is a mystery I never
could fathom. They walk down the street, a chicken tucked under
each arm, as a child might affectionately carry puppies. The fowls,

Harold Nicolson's house
in the Legation
compound, Teheran. He
was born here in 1886
when his father, Sir
Arthur Nicolson, was
British Minister.

too, display a special mentality in this country, for at any street
corner you may see a man squatting beside a brass tray, on which
sit two or more hens beside a couple of dozen eggs in a contented
fashion quite unknown to the hen in England. Even the most
crowded corner of the bazaar does not disturb them. It is equally
likely that on the tray, instead of the hens, you will see a brood of
young partridges, showing no more than the hens a disposition to
stray. Heaven knows that no love of animals prompts this close
and continuous relationship; Persia is no place for a lover of
animals. Indeed, I would rather witness a bull-fight than some of
the scenes I have been treated to in this country. To the skeletons
one very rapidly grows accustomed; that is nothing, a skeleton is
a clean thing. Even to the more recently dead one grows accustomed: to the mule or camel fallen by the wayside, still a rec-
ognisable object, with hairy coat and glazed eyes, the dogs from
the nearest village gorging themselves on its entrails while the
vultures hover, waiting for a nastier meal; this, after the first day
or two (and it is surprising how quickly the sensibility coarsens),
is nothing: one is only glad that the beast should be at last dead,
insentient. It is the living that stir one's horror, one's indignation,
and one's pity. The white horse limping along an endless road; the
team that cannot drag the waggon up the hill, piteously willing
but underfed, overloaded, straining, stumbling, sweating, with
wrung withers and gangrened hocks; the donkey dying under its
load by the roadside, still struggling to rise and carry on a mile or
two farther; why should they serve men as they do serve them,
anxious, faithful, wistful? I remember things that I cannot bring
myself to write. It is not that these people are cruel, but that they
are ignorant; this I do believe, for the Persians are gentle by
inclination, fond of children, and easily moved to laughter in a
simple way. But they seem to be ignorant of suffering; which is as

much as to say, they are childish, they are untaught. It is no uncommon sight to see a man lying on the pavement, vomiting blood or dying of starvation, while all pass him by; yet they are open-handed to their beggars, so long as a man has the strength in him to remain upright and to stretch out his palm. It is simply ignorance and lack of imagination, but the result is the same, and whoever is inclined to grumble against his lot, would do well to remember that he was not born a beast of burden in Persia. It is particularly unfortunate that this country should be so dependent on its beasts, with its vast distances and its lack of transport. It is a country of contradictions; there is nothing to bridge the gulf between the dark ages and the twentieth century; thus, although the postal system between province and province is ramshackle, unreliable, and dilatory in the extreme, you may hear Big Ben

Harold and one
of his dogs, Sally,
in the Legation
grounds.

striking on the wireless in Teheran – with such discrepancy in time that although black night covers Persia, London still basks in a June evening; – news comes to us no later than it flickers round the electric sign in Trafalgar Square; thus, again, though it will take a camel thirty days' good going to carry your merchandise from Teheran to Meshed, you may yourself fly the distance in six hours; it is a country of extremes, one of the few countries where the intervening, that is to say the nineteenth century, conveniences of civilisation will perhaps never be known. Such strange things happen in these forgotten regions of the world. As a consequence, all questions of transport furnish an endless topic of conversation. Whether so-and-so will arrive, or some one else be able to leave; whether he is to be expected on the Wednesday or the Thursday; whether the post will come to-night or not until to-morrow morning, or, indeed, be delayed for a week – all these speculations

form an integral part of life. Are the floods over the Kasvin road?
Has the bridge been swept away again between here and Kum?
Then some one comes into the town with news of the road, and
the information is passed round by word of mouth to all whom it
may concern; and, more or less, and for one reason or another, it
concerns everybody. So you get the curious spectacle of silk-hatted
gentlemen and upholstered ladies engaged in the discussion of these
truly mediæval difficulties. "He is stuck in the mud in the desert,"
you hear; "they sent out an aeroplane for him, but that has stuck
too." The modern and the mediæval jostle in the same phrase. It
is all taken quite as a matter of course.

So we are at the mercy of snow and flood, and also at the mercy
of limp Oriental methods; three cases of wine, despatched from

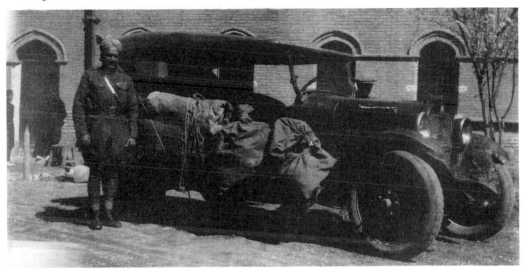

The "bag", containing the Legation's official and private correspondence left Teheran
fortnightly for Bagdad, with the incoming bag "corded onto the splashboards of a
muddy motor". Virginia in Sussex waited about six weeks to receive Vita's reply to one
of her letters.

England in October, have not reached Teheran in May. True, they
were heard of two months ago, about two hundred miles up the
road, but where are they now? Nobody knows. No doubt the
camels came on a patch of green, and have been turned out to
graze. All that we know for certain is that they were once "seen
passing through Hamadan"; the rest is silence. Beyond looking
with interest at every camel I meet lurching along the street, and
trying to read the address upside down on the crate he bears, I
accept this silence with philosophy and drink the amber-coloured
wine of Shiraz instead. The post at least arrives with fortnightly
regularity, corded on to the splashboards of a muddy motor, an
Indian soldier on the box; the headlights stream suddenly down
the road, lighting the white trunks of the plane trees, and then
there is a scramble to sort the letters as some one empties the bags

out on to the table, and every one carries off his budget greedily and jealously, much as a squirrel carries off a nut to his drey. It is almost as hard, in Persia, to believe in the existence of England, as it is, in England, to believe in the existence of Persia; and to piece together, from various letters, what has really been happening to our friends, is like playing a game, or fitting a puzzle: very neat and fascinating, but hard to conceive of as related to any real life. And yet it has its value, for it cuts a new facet on the gem of friendship; to keep in touch with our friends by means of letters only, shows them to us under a new aspect; they are detached, divorced from the apparatus of personality; appearance, voice, gestures are no longer there to mislead and confuse; what we get is an essence, incomplete certainly, and fragmentary, but pure so far as it goes. Then letters become really an enchanting game; we are compelled to contribute all the resources of our imagination; then we find little scraps put away in our memory, little puzzling scraps, that now fall into place, and we enjoy a triumph that at so remote a distance we should yet have made so illuminating a discovery. We shall go back to our friends treading on firmer ground; not, as might be expected, with a gulf between their life and ours.

But this is the exile's pleasure, and it is not to be hoped that those friends in England, with their full life, should have the time to idle over us as we do over them. Yet this, too, may be turned into a satisfaction, for it puts us into the superior position of having found out a number of things while remaining ourselves undiscovered. Sitting on a rock, with the yellow tulips blowing all about me, and a little herd of gazelle moving down in the plain, I dwell with a new intensity on my friends. I know quite well that they are not thinking of me. But they have become my prey, and they are not there to correct or to contradict. It might well be a little alarming for them, this solitary dissection; much more alarming than gregarious gossip, which is bad enough, and makes most people nervous; but fortunately they know nothing about it, so I have the laugh over them. I hold them here, quite tiny, but bright and sharp, in the merciless space of Persia. All old habits of mind have left me, so that it is possible to approach the old ideas with a new eye. The heart is renewed, and winds have blown away the cobwebs.

I had, however, strolled as far as the gate, with no intention of speaking of any of these things, but the amplitude and leisure of the place lead me into discursiveness; there is no hurry, and very little to do except sit and stare. I do not think it a waste of time to absorb in idleness the austere splendour of this place; also I am aware that its colour stains me through and through. Crudely speaking, the plain is brown, the mountains blue or white, the foothills tawny or purple; but what are those words? Plain and

Harold's personal servants in Teheran. Vita captioned this photograph: "(left to right, back row) Bagiar, Regina, Ashpaz; (front row) Zurcha (the saluki) and Taghi holding Henry, Harold's dog"

hills are capable of a hundred shades that with the changing light slip over the face of the land and melt into a subtlety no words can reproduce. The light here is a living thing, as varied as the human temperament and as hard to capture; now lowering, now gay, now sensuous, now tender; but whatever the mood may be, it is superimposed on a basis always grand, always austere, never sentimental. The bones and architecture of the country are there, whatever light and colour may sweep across them; a soft thing passing over a hard thing, which is as it should be. The quality of the light suits this country of great distances. Hills a hundred miles away are clearly scored with the clefts of their valleys, so that their remoteness is unbelievable; Demavend himself, seventy miles distant, looks as though he overhung the town, and might at any moment revive, to annihilate it, his dead volcanic fires. The shapes and promontories of the hills grow familiar: the spur which juts out into the plain near Karedj, the claret-coloured spine of Rhey, the great white backbone at the Elburz, beyond which lie the sub-tropical provinces of the Caspian. They stand with the hardness of an old country; one does not feel that here once swayed the sea, not so very long ago, geologically speaking; on the contrary, this plateau is among the ancient places of the earth, and something of

The snowy Elburz mountains from Doshan Tapeh, a ruined summer palace outside Teheran, which was one of Vita's favourite haunts.

that extreme antiquity has passed into its features, into the jagged profile of its rocks, worn by the weather for untold centuries until it could wear them no more – until it had reduced them to the first shape, and whittled them down to a primal design beneath which it was powerless to delve. Age has left only the bones.

Some complain that it is bleak; surely the rich and changing light removes such a reproach. The light, and the space, and the colour that sweeps in waves, like a blush over a proud and sensitive face. Besides, those who say that it is bleak have not looked, or, looking, have not seen. It is, rather, full of life; but that life is tiny, delicate, and shy, escaping the broader glance. Close and constant observation is necessary, for the population changes from week to week, almost from day to day; a shower of rain will bring out a crop of miniature anemones, a day of hot sun will shrivel them; the tortoises will wake with the warmth; the wasteland stirs. It is necessary to look towards the distance, and then into the few square yards immediately beneath the foot; to be at one and the same time long-sighted and near-sighted.

II

Ever since I have been in Persia I have been looking for a garden and have not yet found one. Yet Persian gardens enjoy a great reputation. Hafiz and Sa-adi sang frequently, even wearisomely, of roses. Yet there is no word for rose in the Persian language; the best they can manage is 'red flower'. It looks as though a misconception had arisen somewhere. Indeed I think the misconception is ours, sprung from that national characteristic by which the English exact that everything should be the same, even in Central Asia, as it is in England, and grumble when it is not.

Vita in the garden of
the British Legation.

'Garden?' we say; and think of lawns and herbaceous borders,
which is manifestly absurd. There is no turf in this parched country;
and as for herbaceous borders, they postulate a lush shapeliness
unimaginable to the Persian mind. Here, everything is dry and
untidy, crumbling and decayed; a dusty poverty, exposed for eight
months of the year to a cruel sun. For all that, there are gardens
in Persia.

The garden of
Farmanieh, later
the summer
residence of the Italian
Ambassador.

But they are gardens of trees, not of flowers; green wildernesses.
Imagine that you have ridden in summer for four days across a
plain; that you have then come to a barrier of snow-mountains

and ridden up the pass; that from the top of the pass you have seen a second plain, with a second barrier of mountains in the distance, a hundred miles away; that you know that beyond these mountains lies yet another plain, and another, and another; and that for days, even weeks, you must ride, with no shade, and the sun overhead, and nothing but the bleached bones of dead animals strewing the track. Then when you come to trees and running

A Persian orchard near Isfahan, "a place of spiritual reprieve, as well as a place of shadows".

water, you will call it a garden. It will not be flowers and their garishness that your eyes crave for, but a green cavern full of shadow, and pools where goldfish dart, and the sound of little streams. That is the meaning of a garden in Persia, a country where the long slow caravan is an everyday fact, and not a romantic name.

Such gardens there are; many of them abandoned, and these one may share with the cricket and the tortoise undisturbed through the hours of the long afternoon. In such a one I write. It lies on a southward slope, at the foot of the snowy Elburz, looking over the plain. It is a tangle of briars and grey sage, and here and there a judas tree in full flower stains the whiteness of the tall planes with its incredible magenta. A cloud of pink, down in a dip, betrays the peach trees in blossom. Water flows everywhere, either in little wild runnels, or guided into a straight channel paved with blue tiles, which pours down the slope into a broken fountain between four cypresses. There, too, is the little pavilion, ruined, like everything else; the tiles of the façade have fallen out and lie smashed upon the terrace; people have built, but, seemingly, never repaired; they have built, and gone away, leaving nature to turn their handiwork into this melancholy beauty. Nor is it so sad as it might be, for in this spacious, ancient country it is not of man that one

thinks; he has made no impression on the soil, even his villages of brown mud remain invisible until one comes close up to them, and, once ruined, might have been ruined for five or five hundred years, indifferently; no, one thinks only of the haven that this tangled enclosure affords, after the great spaces. One is no longer that small insect creeping across the pitiless distances.

There is something satisfying in this contrast between the garden and the enormous geographical simplicity that lies beyond. The mud walls that surround the garden are crumbling, and through the breaches appears the great brown plain, crossed by the three pale roads: to the east, the road to Meshed and Samarcand; to the west, the road to Bagdad; to the south, the road to Isfahan. The eye may travel, or, alternately, return to dwell upon the little grape-hyacinth growing close at hand. These Asian plains are of exceeding beauty, but their company is severe, and the mind turns gratefully for a change to something of more manageable size. The garden is a place of spiritual reprieve, as well as a place of shadows. The plains are lonely, the garden is inhabited; not by men, but by birds and beasts and lowly flowers; by hoopoes, crying "Who? Who?" among the branches; by lizards rustling like dry leaves; by the tiny sea-green iris. A garden in England seems an unnecessary luxury, where the whole countryside is so circumscribed, easy and

Vita leans against a tree overlooking a rare pool in the great plain that surrounds Teheran. Behind her is the Meshed Gap with the road to Samarcand.

secure; but here, one begins to understand why the garden drew such notes from Sa-adi and from Hafiz. As a breeze at evening after a hot day, as a well in the desert, so is the garden to the Persian.

The sense of property, too, is blessedly absent; I suppose that this garden has an owner somewhere, but I do not know who he is, nor can any one tell me. No one will come up and say that I am trespassing; I may have the garden to myself; I may share it with a beggar; I may see a shepherd drive in his brown and black flock, and, sitting down to watch them browse, sing a snatch of the song that all Persians sing at the turn of the year, for the first three weeks of spring. All are equally free to come and enjoy. Indeed there is nothing to steal, except the blossom from the peach trees, and no damage to do that has not already been done by time and nature. The same is true of the whole country. There are no evidences of law anywhere, no sign-posts or milestones to show the way; the caravanserais stand open for any one to go in and rest his beasts; you may travel along any of those three roads for hundreds of miles in any direction, without meeting any one or anything to control you; even the rule of the road is nominal, and you pass by as best you can. If you prefer to leave the track and take to the open, then you are free to do so. One remembers – sometimes with irritation, sometimes with longing, according to the fortunes of the journey – the close organisation of European countries.

The shadows lengthen, and the intense light of sunset begins to spread over the plain. The brown earth darkens to the rich velvet of burnt umber. The light creeps like a tide up the foothills, staining the red rock to the colour of porphyry. High up, above the range of the Elburz, towers the white cone of Demavend, white no longer now, but glowing like a coal; that white loneliness, for ten minutes of every day, suddenly comes to life. It is time to leave the garden, where the little owls are beginning to hoot, answering one another, and to go down into the plain, where the blue smoke of the evening fires is already rising, and a single star hangs prophetic in the west.

III

There is another forsaken palace, of very different aspect, which I frequent. It is on a high, sudden hill, starting up out of the plain; a small hill, whose summit is entirely occupied by those dilapidated buildings, looking from a distance like a tiny Carcassonne. This is Doshan Tapeh – the hill of the hare. It is of the colour of hares, too; rocks pale buff, plaster pale buff, turning pink at sunset. There is no seclusion here; the palace, certainly, has its garden, but it lies at the foot of the hill, quite separate; a walled-in square, symmetrically planted with trees, where Nasr-ed-Din Shah kept his wild animals; but the palace itself, or, rather, the ruins of it,

craggy on its eminence, stands as bare and exposed as the rocks of the surrounding mountains. The views from its broken arcades are magnificent. As the backbone of the north stretches the whole range of the Elburz; to the south-east the Djarjarud hills split dramatically into what is known as the Meshed gap, where the great road crosses on its way to Meshed and Samarcand; to the south and west lies the open plain, bounded only by the very distant mountains beyond Kasvin. Down in the plain lies Teheran, so low and mud-coloured as to be almost invisible, but for the threads of smoke that give it the appearance of some nomad encampment. Never did any capital look less of a capital, even of Persia, partly, I daresay, because it is dwarfed by the immensity in which it lies; yet in fact it is a great rambling place, with its bazaars that wander for miles, breaking now and then into open lanes between mud-walls, but always creeping again beneath vaulted tunnels, like an animal going into its burrow.

Doshan Tapeh still keeps traces of its former splendours. It must have been a gay, coquettish little pavilion, with its bright tiles, columns and arcades, and two terraces, all so airy and high up, the sky and mountains so wide around it. But the ceilings of the poor rooms are all fallen in, and lie in dusty heaps of plaster and tiles on the floor. It is the same story everywhere.

A track leads up to the pavilion, so steep, and crooked with so sharp a bend that surely no carriage can ever have climbed it. Nasr-ed-Din, when he came here, as he often did, for it was his favourite hunting-box, must have ridden, those famous black moustachios of his waving at the head of the cavalcade. Now, the hillside is full of sage and the wild lavender with the big pink flower. I have never yet seen a hare there, though I found a porcupine not so very far off, on the hills behind the tiny Kasr-i-Firouze, where the wild tulips grow, the white ones that are so sweet-scented, and the yellow ones that have no scent at all, but are of a beautiful pure buttercup yellow and of an exquisite clear shape, like a pointed goblet designed by some early draughtsman with a right instinct for line. These wild tulips are very capricious; you may walk for miles without coming upon a trace of them, then suddenly a whole hillside is sprinkled with them, bending and glistening in the sun and the fresh breeze. Nothing more lovely than the natural rock-gardens on these hills, though, to tell the truth, the flowers are disappointing in their limited variety. They make it up, however, in other ways, not least by the genius they display in showing themselves off. When they do this in the obvious way, by coming out into the open and blowing among the stones on narrow ledges, they are charming enough; but when they do it paradoxically, by concealing themselves in a crevice or under a jutting rock, then they are truly enticing and irresistible. One soon gets to know their habits, like the idiosyncrasies of friends; I know that down in the desert I shall find the tiny poppies, red and purple, and the tiny scarlet ranunculus − perhaps, if they were transferred to a more kindly soil, they might grow larger; but when I start to climb I shall come upon the tulips, who like a slope or even a cliff − how rightly! for the sloping ground shows off their straightness better, by contrast, than would the level. The first comer is the native *Iris persica*, which grows indifferently in high and low places, usually in couples, like marriage, one greenish-white, and one bluish-white, a few yards apart, though occasionally you will find a whole family of six or eight, and sometimes a triangular arrangement of three. The yellow squills are everywhere, very strongly scented. The shrubby things interest me less, because I like my flowers small and delicate, − the taste of all gardeners, as their discrimination increases, dwindles towards the microscopic, − but the shrubs have their point too, for they are nearly all pleasantly grey and aromatic. There is one thorny shrub, smothered in spring with pale pink or cherry-pink flowers, which I have not been able to identify; some one told me it was called by the Persians the snow-flower, but as he was wrong about everything else I suspect that he was wrong about this also. It is, at all events, a very pretty thing, making a round bush like a bright pink sponge, about three feet high; it grows in the stoniest ground, apparently independent of water. I wish I were a botanist, instead of a mere dilettante; but do I wish it really? for I am not sure that pure enjoyment does not wane as technical knowledge waxes; I am tempted to put it to the test, by studying botany till I can distinguish Scrophulariaceæ from Caryophyllaceæ, but that I am too much afraid of finding, when I have digested all this knowledge, that I have lost the delights of ignorance. Few delights bear the strain of investigation; they bruise, as tender fruits after handling. It is safer not to know too much. I could scarcely enjoy more than I do at present these random hunts after the flowers of a Persian spring; it does not matter in the least if the day reveals nothing new, for there is always hope round the corner or over the brow of the hill; and the valley where I first found the wild almond, a ravine driven straight into the heart of the mountains, all blossom and tumbling water, was in itself a reward. So one is drawn onward, over miles of country as over reams of paper, and still there is a hill to climb, and still a sentence to write, and no reason why either should ever come to an end, so long as something remains to be discovered beyond. I scarcely know how I have strayed so far from Doshan Tapeh, with Nasr-ed-Din riding up the track, and where now only the innermost room of his palace remains more or less intact, the empty windows gaping towards the northern mountains, and illustrations from the *Illustrated London News* of 1860 papering the walls.

IV

It would seem, however, that Persia is a country made for wandering onward; there is so much room, and no boundaries anywhere, and time is marked only by the sun. Nor is it only in the open country that one wanders, but in the bazaars too, where the Europeans never go, and of which they speak with a surprised contempt. The Europeans like to pretend that they are living in Europe; each European house is a little resolute camp, and any coming and going between house and house is done with closed eyes. If Persia has to be referred to, it is in a tone of grievance, as though the speaker were a martyr condemned for his sins to endure a term of punishment. There are exceptions, but that is the general rule. No doubt there is much that is irritating in Persia; it is irritating not to be able to get a broken blind repaired, or to buy a piece of glass without a bubble in it; irritating to be so much at the mercy of nature in the shape of snow, flood, and mud, impeding our journeys, delaying our posts, and generally interrupting our communications; irritating to see the universal wastage and decay; irritating to hear of corruption and peculation with the elaborate and wearisome system that they involve; but Asia is not Europe, and all countries bestow different gifts. Resignation is essential

The Minister (Sir Percy Loraine) and Harold (centre in the car) leave the Legation for an official visit to the Shah. Vita described the scene to Virginia, "Sir Percy and Harold, both in uniform, with fluttering plumes in their hats, Sir Percy loving it, Harold wretched."

here, if one does not wish to live in a condition of perpetual fury. Then, having emptied the mind of European preconceptions, one is at liberty to turn round and absorb an entirely new set of conditions.

But in the meantime the Europeans go on with their tea-parties, and their leaving of cards, and their speculations as to why some one was not to be seen, yesterday, at some one else's house. How wonderful and perplexing is this system of social intercourse! These people are not friends; they do not, they cannot, enjoy one another's society; there is no intimacy, no truth between them; moreover, no external power condemns them to this treadmill, why then in the name of human liberty do they remain stepping on it until they step themselves off into their graves? The problem is beyond me; I give it up, and stand aside to marvel. For, personally, I prefer the bazaars to the drawing-rooms; not that I cherish any idea that I am seeing 'the life of the people'; no foreigner can ever do that, although some talk a great deal of nonsense about it; but I like to look. It is a harmless taste, and disturbs nobody except myself. Nobody takes any notice of one in the bazaars; certainly far less notice than we should take of a dervish were he to walk down Piccadilly. Even the shopkeepers show no anxiety to sell their wares; one may pause and turn over a bundle of silks, or point, admire, and discuss, without hearing the "Buy! buy!" that assails one in Cairo or Constantinople. Whether this proceeds from the natural apathy of the Persians, or from the fact that they so rarely see tourists, and have not yet learnt about the resources of the tourist's pocket, I do not know. In Cairo the rival merchants tug at one's sleeve: "This is the best shop," they say; "he no good, next door." But the Persians only watch one from under sleepy lids.

The bazaars are vaulted, shadowy, and lit by shafts of sunlight into a Rembrandtesque chiaroscuro. They ramble literally for miles. They are lined with little shops, less shops than stalls. It is impossible to say that one shop is larger than another, though it is possible to say that some are smaller than others. These, the smaller ones, are no bigger than cupboards, mere recesses in the wall; in them squat vendors of shoes – white canvas shoes, with blue rag soles – or old-clothes merchants; henna-dyed beards and

The Indian lancers escorted the Minister, trotting behind and in front of the car.

green turbans among the coloured assortment of rags and tatters. There are the shops hung with harness: tassels, striped nose-bags, bells, scarlet reins with big blue woollen blobs, red saddles. Then there are bazaars devoted to one industry: the leather-workers' street, which is very quiet, industrious, and rich in tone; the coppersmiths' street, filled with the sound as of an army beating on gongs, and resplendent with huge copper trays hanging like shields on the wall, and shelves of silver ewers of the lovely traditional shape seen in sixteenth century miniatures. Very robust and masculine, the red copper; very luminous and feminine the pale silver, shaped like some elegant, paradisaical flower.

But best of all I like the dun-coloured shops where they sell grain, so harmonious and sober in their tonality. The brass scales gleam among the pyramidal heaps of grain; brown, ochre, fawn, neutral, with twine and sacking, and brown men scooping up the wheat in wooden measures. I cannot think of the east as gaudy, but always as brown: earth, and dark skins, the colour of age. How sombre, for instance, are the bazaars; a string of camels passes, laden with bales, or a donkey carrying green vegetables in panniers, a little oil-lamp alight on his back, making an altar of his load, like the sacrifice of Abel.

Darkness is the keynote of this vaulted warren, darkness cleft with sudden beams. The round holes in the roof correspond to the round stains of sunlight on the floor. And it is a darkness not only of fact, but also of impression; a sense of obscure and pullulating life, hurrying about unknown business. Strange, harsh faces pass by; and women secreted behind the eternal veil; women chaffering for bread; but these people, all bent on some practical affair, have their life, their beliefs, their creed, their fanaticism; the bazaar rumours originate amongst them: men, smoking in cafés, talk politics, give credence to extraordinary legends: the Russians have mislaid an army corps somewhere on the frontiers of the Caucasus, the English have organised a plot to assassinate the Shah; all this passes from mouth to mouth; the Persians, who for the most part cannot read, are still great story-tellers, and those stories which do or might affect current events find most favour amongst them. But one does not hear this going on; one is oppressed only by the sense of dark life; then one imagines these separate, hurrying people coagulated suddenly into a mob, pressing forward with some ardent purpose uniting them, and the same intent burning in all those dark eyes.

This is simply an effect of one's own strangeness; there is nothing really sinister about these people. But a life of which one knows nothing, seeing only the surface, does suggest something cabalistic and latent. One is so ignorant oneself, where *they* move with so close a familiarity. To us they are all anonymous, for one thing; but to one another they are named, their fathers are known, they are inter-related; that door in the wall admits you into the house of Hossein the leather merchant, and in the next street lives his brother; their houses are back to back, and in the evening their women meet to gossip on the flat mud roofs. (The story of David, Uriah, and Bathsheba gains in verisimilitude.) How curious a fact it is, that in a strange country, and more especially in the east, one should be so much concerned with the common people; at home one does not (except for more serious purposes) speculate about the secrets of the slums; further, the expressions that one picks first out of a strange language are apt to be expressions of cab-drivers, porters, shopkeepers – as though an Asiatic gentleman travelling in England should pride himself on shouting "Piper!" like a newsboy. Driving a car in the streets of Teheran, I am more tempted to cry "*Havar dar!*" with the muleteers than to use the horn. From the same instinct springs that infuriating habit of authors of sprinkling their pages with foreign words, usually spelt wrong, or used in the wrong connection like *le footing*, *le streughel-feur-lifeur*, or the English heroes and heroines of French novels, Sir Coglowox, and Lady Nonatten. It must come from a sort of snobbishness, a desire to associate oneself, to pretend initiation; but, with literary if not poetic justice, brings its own punishment, for the attempt invariably miscarries. I have a suspicion that I am myself falling into the same trap by this predilection for the bazaars, and wonder whether I should not glance in surprise at a foreigner who aired his enthusiasm for Smithfield market. One has not even the excuse of looking for works of art, for the shops are exceedingly humble, devoted to the necessities of life; there is a pale-blue shop, with silver trays hanging on the walls, and huge bowls of blue glaze, containing 'mast', a sort of curdled milk; a little boy in white stirs the 'mast' with a long spoon; the whole interior is so pale and cool, that to look into it from the dark bazaar is like looking into

A street scene in Teheran. The women wear the *picheh*, a face shade, with their *chador* cloaks.

the milky window of an aquarium. The bread shops are not recessed, but are simply a section of wall, stepped, and on the steps descend the brown blankets of bread, exactly like a drugget laid down a staircase; you buy the bread by weight, and carry it away thrown over your arm like a travelling-rug.

Then the bazaars are full of surprises; in one place it is a sword stuck up to the hilt into the wall, Rustem's sword, they say, Rustem being their favourite heroic character; and in another place it is an open courtyard, shaded by large trees, where one can buy all kinds of junk, laid out in little chess-board squares on the ground, for a few farthings, every kind of thing from old sardine-tins to silver kettles pawned by Russian refugees. Nothing more tragic than this evidence of the Russian catastrophe; here is an old gramophone record, and here a pair of high button boots, very small in the foot, with a pair of skates screwed on; they speak, not only of present-day personal misery, but of a life once lived in gaiety; and all theoretical sympathy with Lenin vanishes at the sight of this human, personal sacrifice made on the altar of a compulsory brotherhood. Russia seems very near. Indeed, in Asia the different countries do seem nearer to one another, more mingled, than do different countries in Europe, by some contradiction, despite the enormous distances; here in Persia one cannot lose sight of the fact that China, Russia, Turkestan, Arabia, surround us, remote though they may be, and buried each in a separate darkness; perhaps because vagrants from out of these neighbouring regions find their way to the Persian bazaars, and wander with an air of strangeness, in different clothes that proclaim the country of their origin, an Arab in his burnous, a Russian in his belted shirt, a Turcoman in his shaggy busby, unlike Europeans, who differ from one another, if at all, only by their complexions. In the open courtyard of the bazaars, the green field as it is called, nationalities jostle, poking amongst the junk-stalls for some scrap of treasure, a buckle, or a collar-stud, while the vendors squat near at hand, with lacklustre eye, less concerned to sell than to see that nothing is stolen.

Such a desultory life I lead, and the life of England falls away, or remains only as an image seen in an enchanted mirror, little separate images over which I pore, learning more from them than ever I learnt from the reality. I lead, in fact, two lives; an unfair advantage. This roof of the world, blowing with yellow tulips; these dark bazaars, crawling with a mazy life; that tiny, far-off England; and what am I? and where am I? That is the problem: and where is my heart, home-sick at one moment, excited beyond reason the next? But at least I live, I feel, I endure the agonies of constancy and inconstancy; it is better to be alive and sentient, than dead and stagnant. "Let us", I said, as we emerged from the bazaars, "go to Isfahan."

CHAPTER VI

TO ISFAHAN

I

KINGLAKE, who was a good excitable traveller although his patches may have been a trifle too purple (but that was the fashion of his day), makes an excellent observation about eastern travel. His route lay then through mere Serbia, but in the middle of the nineteenth century, so that what he lost in geographical advantage was compensated by historical difficulty of progress. "The actual movement from one place to another", he says, "in Europeanised countries is a process so temporary – it occupies, I mean, so small a proportion of the traveller's entire time, that his mind remains unsettled so long as the wheels are going; he may be alive enough to external objects of interest, and to the crowding ideas which are often invited by the excitement of a changing scene, but he is still conscious of being in a provisional state, and his mind is for ever recurring to the expected end of his journey; his ordinary ways of thought have been interrupted, and before any new mental habits can have been formed he is quietly fixed in his hotel. It will be otherwise with you when you journey in the east. Day after day, perhaps week after week, and month after month, your foot is in the stirrup. To taste the cold breath of the earliest morn, and to lead or follow your bright cavalcade till sunset through forests and mountain passes, through valleys and desolate plains, all this becomes your MODE of LIFE, and you ride, eat, drink, and curse the mosquitoes as systematically as your friends in England eat, drink, sleep. If you are wise you will not look upon the long period of time thus occupied in actual movement as the mere gulf dividing you from the end of your journey, but rather as one of those rare and plastic seasons of your life from which, perhaps, in after times, you may love to date the moulding of your character – that is, your very identity. Once feel this, and you will soon grow happy and contented in your saddle home." How right was Kinglake! as right as when he speaks, in another place, of the "testing of the poet's words by map and compass". Not until I had experienced what he had experienced, did I really appreciate his full meaning. As to copy out a passage, in one's own handwriting, in the slow and detailed process of script, is to weigh the value of words and to extract (from what might have seemed a cursory phrase) the heavier significance of a careful, measured statement, so to adopt the MODE of LIFE is to enter personally into the full significance of that life. It is true that I had not, as had Kinglake, to accommodate myself to the stirrup and the "saddle home", but only to the driving-seat of a Ford car; but even so the familiarity of the method became a part of me, as surely as the loading of his pack-horse became a part of Kinglake; by the end of the first day it had become instinctive in me to glance over the side to see whether the corded petrol-tins had slipped, or whether the canvas bags that held our bedding still retained their slant along the mud-guard; each object of necessity had its place: the enamel washing-basin that was for ever getting mixed up, under my feet, with the clutch-pedal and the brake, the big sheepskin that was now ungratefully tossed into the back, now dragged forward as the wind whistled over the draughty passes. A remarkable amount of stuff can be packed on to a motor if you know how to do it and don't mind about the paint. The example of the Persians teaches one this, for they treat a motor exactly as though it were a pack-animal. For generations they have been accustomed to heap their camels and their donkeys with various merchandise, desisting only when the animal's legs actually begin to give way, and so with their new,

On the road to Isfahan.

swifter beast of burden they desist from their loading only when the springs begin to grate and the tyres to flatten. You meet upon the road objects which the average English chauffeur would scarcely recognise as motor-cars. The poor little Fords almost disappear under the huge bales that swell out over the mudguards; and then, as though that were not enough, eight or nine men crowd on to the motor that was built for five; they perch on the bales as sparrows on a hay-stack, squat in the hood, and are not above sitting astride the bonnet. Even then the pedestrian as they overtake him will cheerfully hail the car and ask for a lift; and he, too, hitches himself on somehow, and the unwieldy affair goes off again, driven at its top speed always, regardless of bumps and ditches. We ourselves travelled after the Persian fashion, independent of food and even, at a pinch, of lodging, with camp beds and blankets,

food in knapsacks, water-bottles packed into a green canvas
bucket; and very pleasant was the resulting sense of freedom, all the finicky clutter of ordinary life and unnecessary possessions cleared away. It was indeed one of those "rare and plastic seasons", not to be measured in time – for we were only four days and nights on the road – but by a clearing of the spirit, an alteration of material values, a liberation.

II

We had intended to start three days earlier, but a fall of snow delayed us. Such a fall, we were assured, had never been known before in April; and indeed the effect was very strange: irises, wistaria, lilac, roses, in full flower, weighted down by the white load, one season trespassing on another season, winter on spring. The Elburz, whose snows had been rapidly shrinking up towards the summit, appeared suddenly white again one morning; Demavend, whose lower slopes had been streaked with darker ground, again presented a smooth white surface. Such snow meant floods, for it would melt as quickly as it had come. Some people returning from Isfahan reported floods on the road; they had been driving all night, and arrived at four in the morning, drenched with blizzard, half dead with anxiety and fatigue; they advised delay. Such delays and modifications of plan, due to a sudden anger of nature, were too common to be accepted with anything but resignation: we waited two days, till the snow shrank again on the hillside and the earth was brown.

Leaving Teheran at dawn, through the streets still fresh from the efforts of the water-men, who in their unscientific but efficacious way fling the contents of jugs and pails (even of saucepans) across the road, scooped out from the stream in the gutter, we came presently to Kum, its great gold mosque gleaming brilliant above a field of young wheat. We had crossed nearly a hundred miles of strange, desolate country. Curious geological formations twisted the landscape into a sort of dead-world scenery; so might appear regions of the moon, and quite as lifeless, but for the blue jays and the blue-and-orange bee-eaters, and an occasional brown vulture who spread his wings and flapped away in that flight which is so ungainly near the ground, and so noble when risen to the heights where he properly belongs. We had experienced that sensation so common in Persia, of topping a ridge of hills and of looking down over a new stretch of country, not exactly a plain in this instance, for it was always a plain broken by many accidents; broken by those strange rocks which seemed to advance in battalions, like the dreams of some mad painter, not beautiful, but curious and freakish, and lending themselves to wild resemblances in the imagination. Now it seemed that a regiment of giant tortoises advanced, evil under the cliff of their shells; now like murderous

engines of war a promontory of rocks threatened, frozen in their array; now the monotonous brown was stained by a crimson cliff, and now by a patch of sick-turquoise green, as though some sinister chemical had been sprayed upon it.

Then we came beyond that region, and topped its further boundary, and saw below us the salt lake, shimmering like an opal, milky and wide, looking innocent of the many caravans swallowed by its quicksands. There was scarcely a dwelling in all those miles, once we had passed the oasis of Shah Abdul Azim and the swamps of Hassanabad, till we came to Kum, where the wheat was springing, and the mosque rose out of the wheat across the river; but we could not stop at Kum, and pressed onward again, after filling our eyes with the beauty of the great gold dome so rounded above the brown roofs and the green fertility of the fields. We pressed forward, and the landscape changed; we were on the high plateaux now, and the hills were sharper; snow reappeared on their peaks, and the deep blue shadows again carved their flanks. Once more we had climbed to the roof of Asia. And now we were accompanied by a familiar and yet an unfamiliar spectacle: the cone of Demavend which, seen as a daily companion from Teheran, had taken his place merely as a mountain among the other mountains, but which, seen now from a distance of over a hundred miles, so overtopped his fellows that on discovering him we stared incredulous. There he was, so distant and so enormous; so high, that at first we

thought a cloud had aped his contours. Then, as the sun sank, we saw his base cut off by some effect of the light, so that the cone alone remained, detached, smooth, and white, but presently flushed to pink – a pink island floating in the blue. We were travelling away from him, but for a long time he remained, a red beacon in the north, till darkness came, and he silently and mysteriously disappeared.

Meanwhile we had had enough to look at in our immediate surroundings, without turning our heads to watch Demavend like a red flamingo flying across the sky, for the sunset on our high lonely plateau had excelled itself in beauty. Lonely, indeed, for we passed only a shepherd with his flock, or a single horseman crossing the plain on his way to some village on the hills. But for these – who had been immemorially the same – such sunsets as we now beheld had spilt themselves out unnoted since first that very ancient portion of the earth hardened after the primeval convulsions into its definite forms. We were seizing only one moment out of all that prodigality; yet dawn continues to break over those Asian heights while England still lies in sleep, and sunset stains those hills while England works in the full activity of afternoon. At three o'clock I may think of the hills turning red on the east, and in the west deepening to blue under a yellow sky, in a loneliness as great as that which reigned before the world was peopled.

An hour after dark we came to Dilijan, which we had begun to

The road to Isfahan crosses a plain which to Vita was "a very ancient portion of the earth hardened after the primeval convulsions into its definite forms".

think existed on the map but not elsewhere, and, turning aside from the road, made our way up narrow lanes between the mud walls to the house of the village headman. The moon was risen by now, casting deep shadows, lighting up little courtyards through

At Dilijan, where the English party slept one night on their way to Isfahan, with their host the village headman.

the black span of arches. The village was like a walled city of the Middle Ages, as labyrinthine, and as secret. A couple of men ran before us, showing the way, and stopped us before an arched entrance; this was the headman's house, where we should be given a room for the night. The house, more or less tumble-down, surrounded a courtyard after the manner of all Persian houses; a lake of moonlight lay across the middle of the court, and in a dark corner crouched the figures of women round an open brazier. The room we were given was plain and clean, whitewashed, with three arches opening on to the court. It contained no furniture, only rows of lamps and teapots standing in the alcoves. We sat in the arches, smoking, content with silence, and feeling that a long journey in time as well as in space separated us in this moonlight of a lost Persian village from the dawn that had seen our departure from Teheran. Journeys by train give no intimacy with the country crossed, no such intimacy as that which comes from following a road in all its miles, stopping now as a patch of flowers by the wayside hails the attention, stopping again to eat and drink under the shadow of a rock, sitting on the ground and watching the vultures wheel or the insects run, startling a hare from its form, becoming for a moment identified with a spot remote and unfrequented, which has a life of its own, and which in all probability one will never see again.

III

Next morning the lakes and shadows of moonlight had gone, but lakes and shadows of sunlight, more brilliant and no less deep, had taken their place. The women were busy spinning in the courtyard. Skeins of scarlet and yellow wool hung in the arches; and with scarlet handkerchiefs tied round their heads the women squatted on the step, the spindles twirling beneath their practised hands. I photographed them, and they besieged me, asking to see the result, but I had to explain that they must wait at least three weeks before the post-cart would bring the pictures. They seemed disappointed, and none too confident that the promised photographs would ever arrive; but whether it was me, or, with better reason, the post-cart that they mistrusted, I do not know.

We wandered out, along the twisting lanes of the village between the high brown walls, and coming round a corner found ourselves suddenly on the plain. From here the village looked more like a walled city than ever, with its gate cut darkly in the wall, and

Dilijan in the morning, when Vita photographed the women spinning in the courtyard.

several little towers like barbicans, and the absence of windows or other openings, giving the impression of a fortified place. All was brown and blue; brown plain, brown village, blue sky, and in the distance blue hills faintly streaked with snow. But it was not deserted, for under the wall walked a file of young women, six or eight of them, a few yards apart, each with a distaff in her hand, up and down a long trail of wool between wooden pegs on the ground; and each as she went added the strand from her distaff to the trail, holding it down with a forked stick, in and out amongst the pegs, like a sort of cat's-cradle. What the object of this occupation was, I cannot conceive, since the wool on the distaffs was not ravelled, and, having unwound it thus and laid it out upon the ground, I cannot see what there remained for them to do but to wind it all up again. However, that was their concern, and in the meantime they provided a very pleasant and surprising sight; and a sight also very satisfying, in its suggestion of placid, primitive labour, which seemed to fall naturally into its place among the occupations of the men, with their rude ploughs and pastoral idle days. A great repose it afforded to the mind, this simple community, growing a little wheat, breeding lambs and kids enough for flesh and skins, weaving the cloth for their own covering; so self-sufficient, and so far removed from the vile ambitions of industry. It was like a return to a fresher world, there under the wall of Dilijan in the early morning; a world which, plus the existence of a doctor and a dispensary, might fairly have been called ideal. And since I was determined to go through Persia with an eye to outward appearances only, ignoring the physical disease and political corruption which were not my province and which I could do nothing to alleviate, to my fancy it *was* ideal, though that might be a shallow way of looking at it.

The road from Dilijan lay across a plain thick with asphodel, which ceased as abruptly as it had begun, as is the patchy fashion of all plant life in Persia. Conditions do not seem to alter, to explain this capriciousness on the part of the flowers, but there it is: either they grow or they do not grow, and there is an end of it. Mulleins, too, which habitually favour a damp soil, had sprinkled themselves over this arid plain, but they had chosen badly, for poor starved dusty things they were, looking as though they would shrivel long before the moment came for them to throw up their yellow spires. We were on the high tablelands, at a height of perhaps six thousand feet, so that the hills which ran parallel to our course, bordering the plain, kept the snow on their jagged summits, inconsiderable though their rise appeared to be. This, we agreed, as we bundled along over the endless, bumpy road, was the type of landscape which above all gave the effect of Central Asia. To be so high that, although the sun was powerful, the region of snow seemed but so very little higher; to breathe air of that

A village on the road to Isfahan: "Sometimes we would come on a little oasis of green . . . with a handful of mud houses."

incomparable purity; to have the sensation of being on the roof; to detect, beyond the range of near hills, a farther, bluer range; so must Tibet look, and so Pamir. We had, too, those vast high solitudes to ourselves, mile after mile, plain after plain, – for we crossed many low cols, scarcely to be called passes, which always opened out again a view of plain as extensive as the one we had just conquered. A heartbreaking country, indeed, to ride across, when each view ahead meant a day's journey for a horse. Yet it must not be thought that the journey was monotonous, for sometimes we would come on a little oasis of green, – the brilliant green of young wheat, and straight poplar trees just broken into leaf above a stream, – with a handful of mud houses, and sometimes an abrupt change led us into a gorge as dire and dark as the inferno, but always the view opened again, on to plateau and mountains, and the long straight road leading for twenty, thirty miles ahead.

And although the plains were desert land, they were as good as watered by large and frequent (though always distant) lakes, with reedy edges, and the snowy reflections of mountain tops mirrored in their shimmering surface. Indeed, in some places the mountains rose as islands out of the lake, as fantastic as the strange landscapes of Leonardo, and as rocky, and of as deep a blue. Sometimes the lake appeared straight ahead, lying across the road, and cutting off the base of the solid hills, so that they floated unsubstantially; and even dwindled in size, till they finally went out, like a blown candle – but reappeared again, growing from little shapeless puffs in the heart of the mirage to their own rocky form, still detached, still ethereal, but joining up with their fellows as we advanced towards them, till once more a coherent range barred the plain. Sometimes the lake lay to the left hand or the right, either at the foot of the hills, when it spread wide and placid, reflecting peaks and sky with disconcerting conviction, or cutting off the base of the hills, as a sea-coast skirting the edge of a fabulous, pinnacled

"We had those vast high solitudes to ourselves, mile after mile, plain after plain ... where rose tier after tier of blue jagged crests."

A shepherd on the way to
Isfahan.

country, where rose tier upon tier of blue jagged crests, resting (as
it seemed) upon nothing, in an extravagance of lovely unreality. It
created, to the eye, a world of myth where substance and illusion
floated together in romantic marriage; all the more romantic for
the knowledge that it would never again be exactly repeated, never
exactly the same distortion, the same association of mist and light,
concealment and revelation. A brief world, of changing shapes,
hinting at ravines and caverns, pools and lagoons running up
into the hills, all magical, all inhabited by nymphs and monsters,
chimeras, wyverns, and fabulous Circean beings; a world of grot-
toes and blue profundities, of reflections doubly deceptive, since
neither the mirror nor the image was really there; a world which
we, and we alone, might see, perpetually shifting, changing, and
recreated. There is a picture in Venice, by Bellini I think, in which
Venus sitting in a boat is drawn or at any rate accompanied by
cherubim swimming in the green waters round her feet, while
behind her rises a blue landscape of just such a world, all in an
unearthly daylight which shall not be called submarine, but rather
the light of watery caves; such a world, such a light, we saw, all
close at hand though we could never hope to reach it, could never
wander into its enchanting fastnesses or gaze into those false and
limpid mirrors which might have given back, like the looking-glass
in the fairy story, the reflection of distant events or the face of the
beloved; for surely there must exist in some desert country of the
world a legend that he who looks into the waters of a mirage will
behold there an image hidden to all other eyes? These waterless,
watered plains seem a very breeding-ground for superstition. Other
manifestations we saw, such as the dust-demons which, at a little
distance, rose like djinns in a column and swirled away, not
obeying the direction of the wind as we conceived it to be, but

hurrying off in opposite ways, as though following their own wishes, independent of the more explicable wishes of nature.

We found no shade anywhere that day, so we ate our luncheon in a ruined caravanserai, the broken arches framing the peaks of snow and the blue sky, then packed ourselves in again, and after about two hours of travelling, accompanied now by swarms of butterflies, whose little shadows danced along in the dust beside us, passed over a little col, and saw before us, on the farther edge of the new plain, two blue domes swelling over a wash of green. The road became very soft and sandy; that last bit of the journey seemed the longest bit of all. At last we came to melon fields, and fields of opium poppies, and began to pass peasants either labouring in the fields or driving their donkeys towards the town, and before we knew it we were between walls, and then in a crowded street, and at the end of the street lay the Meidan of Isfahan.

The Meidan of Isfahan, which in 1926 still preserved intact the vast open space constructed in the 18th. century as a polo-ground.

IV

It is very rash to go to Isfahan. It is wiser to keep the cities of beautiful name for mental pilgrimage only; "not in Bokhara nor in Samarcand nor in Balkh . . ." says the Persian poet, who, like Milton and Marlowe and not a few other poets, evidently had a weakness for the romantic names. But really it is quite safe to go to Isfahan; for it lies at the foot of its hills in the heart of Persia, as true to its name now as it was in the times of Hajji Baba, whose adventures should be carried in the pocket. All the protagonists of Morier's story jostle in the streets: the scribe, the beggar, the seller of water, the woman in the white veil, the merchant riding on his

The entrance to the bazaar, Isfahan, where it was possible to walk more than three miles under cover without retracing your steps.

horse with his apprentice mounted behind him. In the Meidan a dervish was sitting on the ground telling a story to the crowd; they sat round him in a circle with lips parted and eyes popping nearly out of their heads as the holy man worked himself up into a state of frenzy over the exploits of his hero (for Persian stories are usually heroic, and Firdusi's epic of the Kings their favourite recital). With his long beard, high hat, and orange nails, and fierce little eyes flashing out of his hairy face, he seemed indeed wild and inspired, as though he had been spinning his tale for the last five hundred years and was only now working up to the climax. It was evening, the Meidan was sparsely populated; only a few idlers strolled, men in long robes, hems raising a little swirl of dust; they paced, as students might pace a cloister, hands clasped behind their backs, heads bent, gravely conversing. At one end of the vast Meidan rose the blue gateway and turquoise dome of the mosque; at the other end gaped the entrance to the dark bazaars: religion and cupidity facing one another. Fanaticism, barter, dusk and the storyteller, all gathered together, in this eastern city. The graceful little Ali Carpi, midway, was like a flower in the dusk. I could not

Isfahan: the Meidan and Ali Carpi, an archway crowned by an immense columned balcony which formerly served as an audience hall.

believe that I was in Isfahan; it seemed too improbable to be true. "Jousted in Aspramont or Montalban ..." There were the stone goal-posts, near the vaulted entrance to the bazaars; for the Meidan was once a polo-ground. There was the dervish, still churning up the turmoil of his story; a horseman had drawn rein, and sat in the saddle, listening; he carried a long upright lance, stuck into his stirrup. Some one had lit a brazier, which produced strange effects of shadow amongst the crowd, and threw a fitful light on to the face of the dervish. The guttural language spurted as though in ecstasy from his lips. He jerked his hands in wild gesticulation.

But all around, in the twilight that encircled that focus of glow
and frenzy, the Meidan lay like a lake of peace, long, narrow, level;
and within the entrance to the bazaars a single lantern burned,
showing the way into that obscure and unfathomable warren.

v

I climbed next day to the roof of the Ali Carpi, and looked
enviously across the roofs of the city towards the south, where the
road went up the hill to Shiraz and Persepolis. I had no time to go
to Shiraz and Persepolis that April, but it was a pleasure deferred,
not a pleasure foregone; simply something to be put off till next
year, so I gazed enviously but without bitterness, and then turned
to gaze towards the jagged Bakhtiari hills, which I should cross
next year also, on foot with a little convoy of mules to carry my tent
and luggage. All this gave me an agreeable sense of anticipation; it
was agreeable also to feel that I should be in Isfahan once more,
for it is very poignant to say to oneself, "I shall never see this place
again". There must, however, I thought, be something a little
wrong with some one who attached, instinctively, so much import-

ance to place; it betrayed a spiritual superficiality, too material an
attitude; I had thought to gain emancipation by tearing myself up
from my roots, and here I was already netted in the love of Persia.
Worse than that, – for love of Persia was after all an understandable
and reasonable thing, – worse than that, I had caught myself
suffering real little pangs all along the way; even crossing India,
when I saw a road, wanted to travel down it, and had to remember
that that road with its turns and stretches would be gone from me
for ever in a flash. These brief but frequent fallings-in-love gave
me cause for serious anxiety; such vibrations of response ought, I
felt, to be reserved for one's contact with human beings, nor should
nature have a greater power than human nature to excite and to
stir the soul. That disposition might make a good traveller but
surely it made also a bad, an inadequate, friend? The external
world had too much importance for me; my appreciation was

Isfahan: from the roof of
the Ali Carpi one looks
across to the royal
mosque, built in the 15th.
century and covered in
brilliantly enamelled
tiles.

altogether too painfully vivid; but as I meditated, looking over the roofs of Isfahan, I knew that there was no help for it: those hills, that Shiraz road, squeezed my heart as in a muscular hand. I was a victim, and could escape from myself no more than any other

Isfahan: the Chel Setun, one of the pavilions set in the garden of the royal palace and famous as the throne-room of Shah Abbas.

slave of temperament. Only, it was a form of temperament for which I could expect very little sympathy or understanding; an absurdity, an exaggeration. Better to keep it private, – but in a book consecrated to my weakness, that would present some little difficulty.

Ali Carpi trembled under my feet; at first I thought that an earthquake was about to level Isfahan in one magnificent cloud of dust, but soon realised that the trembling was due merely to the insecurity of the frail old building. So I remained where I was. I could look down into the tank of the Hall of Forty Columns – the Chel Setun – fringed with umbrella pines and ending squarely at the foot of the little palace. I could look down into the Meidan, where the tiny figures strolled, or a carriage like a toy crossed the square followed by a swirl of dust. I could look almost into the courtyard of the mosque – that sanctuary forbidden to the unbeliever. To look down upon a city from a roof high above its roofs is to gain a new aspect; everything appears at an odd angle, and freakish framings make little complete pictures like the vignettes in mediæval paintings; thus between the blue domes I got a group of brown houses, with the profile of the hills behind; or through the ogives of a window I got one rounded bubble of blue dome, like a huge mappemonde, the continents and seas represented by the stains where the tiles had fallen off. There was

plenty to amuse an idler on the roof, and to descend from those
airy solitudes to the earth below was like coming down into a world
of which one had taken wily advantage, gained a surreptitious and
almost dishonourable acquaintance.

Friends in Isfahan, cap-
tioned by Vita: (back
row) Raymond
Mortimer, Mrs Bristow,
Gladwyn Jebb; (front
row) Vita, Harold,
Captain Wickham.

VI

Perched up on their scaffolding in a dark whitewashed barn of the
bazaars, the carpet-makers threaded their spindles, sitting with
dangling legs twenty feet above ground before the stretched warp
and woof of the carpet. They sat in a row, as swallows on a
telegraph wire, ten or twelve of them, weaving with the quick
hands of practice. Little boys in round cashmere caps, young men
in blue linen, they presented a row of backs, and of crossed feet
swinging in long, pointed, white canvas shoes, and as they wove
they chattered, pulling at the coloured wools, knocking the stitches
down into place, leaning forward, reaching for another skein. As
the eyes grew accustomed to the darkness, the rich texture of the
carpet emerged in blues and reds; like a half-lived life, stretched
on its frame, the pattern of the lower half was clear, but the upper
half still rose naked, the brown strings waiting for the daily inch
of the design. Shafts of sunlight speared the room, shooting down
from holes in the roof, and quivering in circles on the floor. In a
corner stood a great wooden framework, a rude primitive con-
trivance of stays, rollers, and pulleys, laced with twine; squatting
in front of this, three women, veritable Parcae, spun the wool on
to distaffs. The heavy woollen skeins hung like clusters of fruit; as

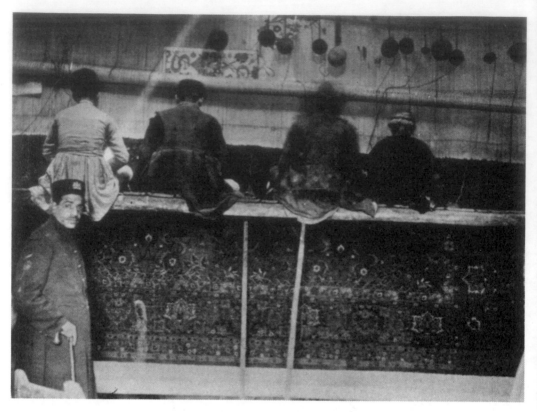

Carpet-making, Isfahan.

red as pomegranates, as blue as grapes, as yellow as lemons; they jumped and bobbed with the spinning; the roughened fingers ran up and down the drawn-out strands, robbing them of their beard, before the quick twist spun them up into the conical ball on the distaff. The women looked up with a grin: here was something that they could do better than the superior foreigner. All their lives (I supposed) they had known, day in, day out, this rasp of the wool between their fingers, until, for them, it became the one physical sensation intimately known; the one habitual thing that would trudge through their half-dreams between sleeping and waking. But they were unaware that I supposed this; nor, being aware, would they have cared or understood, any more than the Egyptian potters, for life is rough and practical, and there is no time for those finer shades that delight the idle. An unchanged, traditional industry; that rude barn enshrined all the quality of the ancient crafts, in essence the same as the carpenter's shop, the forge, the wine-press; full of the clumsy laborious processes of such immemorial trades, but rich in a spirit denied to the apter methods of convenience. The art of carpet-making is not dead in Persia. Not only does it thrive in Isfahan, but in the tents of the nomad tribes the women weave, according to the traditional pattern of their province; they weave for their own use, and for the markets, keeping the hereditary skill alive, on the hillside and by the fires. How many people, in England, look intelligently at

the rug they trample? How many people, who peer into a picture
or examine a chair, will bring an equal fastidiousness to bear upon
a carpet? Yet a carpet is a work of art with a special chance of
appealing to even the most general taste; it is no otiose ornament,
but a necessity, and furthermore, by its symmetry of design it
panders to the human predilection for a repeated pattern. It can
share either the flat quality of fresco, or the deep opulence of
texture. For all that, it is neglected save by a few, and even by
those few it is liable to be maltreated and hung upon a wall, which
is not the proper place for a carpet.

I grew angry as I watched the weavers and thought of these
things, and angrier still remembering the degenerate taste of the
Persians themselves, who, for all the fine tradition behind them,
will treat a carpet as though it were a picture, not only by hanging
it on the wall, but by causing actual pictures to be reproduced, as
fights between archers, or cherubs floating in an orange grove, or
young women pouring libations for their lovers. These productions
they esteem, and display with pride, taking the Oriental's delight
in ingenuity. I remembered how in Constantinople, before the war,
when everything flowed by that channel from out of Asia on its
way to the European markets, it had been possible to spend a
whole afternoon in a shop, lounging, while one rug more beautiful
than the last was unrolled, dusky, faded, the treasures of sixteenth-
century Isfahan. Now, although nothing new has taken the place
of the old – yet the possibilities of pattern are infinite – and
although by instinct the weavers in the tents and villages keep to
the safe tradition, the Europeans neglect the ancient art, and the
richer Persians corrupt the modern product so far as they are able.
The workers alone have not gone wrong. Craftsmen do not go
wrong. That which is made by the hand, built up in an intimate
relationship between creation and maker, lives by a life of its own
so long as it is not interfered with by pretentious meddlers. I came
out, indignant, into the sun.

VII

But by far the most lovely thing I saw in Isfahan, one of those
things whose loveliness endures as a melody in the mind, was the
Madrasseh, meaning school; but if a school at all, then a school
for pensiveness, for contemplation, for spiritual withdrawal; a
school in which to learn to be alone. A cloister, not in the archi-
tectural sense of the word, but in the psychological; a place of
retreat and harmony, open to all, but where each one might go in
a privilege of privacy, to sit or to pace, or to gaze into the water, to
arrive or to depart, unnoticed, unquestioned, in that independence
which few communities understand or are willing to accord. One
is allowed to be lonely there; but in more civilised communities no
one is allowed to be lonely; the refinement of loneliness is not

The Madrasseh, Isfahan, built in 1710 as a college for mullahs. Curzon wrote that it was one of the stateliest ruins he saw in Persia.

understood. Was it the mere visual beauty of the place? or the atmosphere, the very air, soaked in spiritual experience, that produced this profound impression? Certainly the visual beauty was very great, and, aware that I was all too apt to be led astray by such outward seductions, I examined my impressions severely: still, after all the paring away, remained such convictions as I had known only in monasteries and cloisters, places where men had chosen a secluded (perhaps a cowardly) life; a sense that each man had, indeed, a private existence, moments in which it was necessary that he should be apart, for a little, from his fellows. The Madrasseh of Isfahan differed in this from the monastery, that it was the refuge of men ordinarily engaged in worldly affairs; merchants, traders, scholars, pilgrims, came here alike, for an hour, for a day; no conventions were binding; those who chose to be alone, might be alone, walking apart; those who chose might drift into a little group, talking of current politics; those who would pray, might pray; but all were respected, in the indulgence of their several needs. As to the outward beauty of this place: a long range of buildings, tiled in blue, enclosed a rectangular space; a long pool, with steps going down into the water, reflected the buildings; lilac and irises, in sheets of purple, seemed but a deeper echo of the colours of the tiles; a golden light of sunset struck the white trunks of the plane trees, flushing them until they turned to living flesh; and among the lilacs, the irises, and the planes strolled the tall, robed figures, or sat by the water's edge, idly stirring the water with the point of a stick, so that the reflections quivered to a cloud of amethyst and blue, then steadied again to mirror in glassy stillness the blue walls, the spreading leaves, the evening sky.

CHAPTER VII

KUM

AT evening we came again to Kum, that sacred place, this time driving into the town, and being swallowed up almost immediately under the dark arch of the bazaars. We were tired, after a run of nearly two hundred miles, and had yet to find a lodging; we drove to a house we knew of, and beat on the door, but although a dog barked inside, no one came to open. The usual crowd collected – little boys scribbled with their fingers in the dust that whitened the car – beggars whined and stretched out their hands – the black veiled women stood and stared and whispered – then our servant asked, would we honour the house where he was born? But how to find the house? for he had forgotten the way. Volunteers surged forward, perched themselves heaven knows how on the luggage, crouching on the splashboards, hanging on like monkeys, holding on with one hand and wildly waving the other; so we moved off again, and plunged into the bazaar, cleaving our way very slowly through that busy hour of dusk, when the whole population comes out to buy and talk, and the donkeys are driven in from the country with their loads of camel-thorn, and everybody shouts, – and shouted all the more, at the unusual sight of a motor in that place. It was dark, only a few little shop-lamps burnt, making tiny shrines of light at intervals down the street; I switched on my headlights, and their beam rushed down the bazaar, a fierce and concentrated illumination, leaving the donkeys to jostle in the shadows with their great loads, and only a soft bump to tell us that we had hit a pack as we squeezed our way through. Our volunteers guided us well, down alleys and round corners; our servant meanwhile in a great state of delight, balancing himself on the step at an acrobatic angle, beating off the children with sound whacks of an umbrella. I was not sorry to emerge from the bazaars, before we had run over anybody, into the open street, and to see again the sky over our heads and to be rid of that jostling, shouting, hailing crowd. The street was so narrow that the car could just pass between the mud walls, lurching from rut to rut, the steering wheel half twisted out of my hands. A score of boys straggled after us, holding on to the car and shouting. Then we came to a cross-street, and drew up at the corner house; the news of our arrival had travelled quicker than we had; the door was already open, our host was greeting us – a tall, black-bearded man of incomparable dignity – and eager hands were loosening the cords that secured our luggage.

After noise, silence; after movement, stillness. A little house round a courtyard; the rectangular tank reflecting the pale sky; a bush of oleander; a room, carpeted, but bare of furniture. Are these things worth chronicling? Probably not. But of such arrivals and such transitory hours, – of such glances through a door once opened and then forever shut, – journeys in Persia are made. I remember the chicken they cooked for us, in the juice of pomegranates and walnuts, and the huge dish of golden rice. I remember

the sensation of stretching tired limbs on a pile of rugs. I remember asking our host if he could play the *tar* (for many Persians chant the poets, striking a few chords on the strings of their native instrument), and his producing instead a discordant gramophone with half a dozen scratchy records, which out of politeness we were compelled to play. I remember night falling on the little court, and sleep falling on our eyelids.

Kum, a stronghold of the Shia faith and containing many tombs of saints, visited on the way back to Teheran from Isfahan.

II

Then in the morning the house basked in a soft, hot brilliance; a woman knelt to wash her rags in the tank; pigeons cooed on the roof; a baby toddled out; a dog flopped down in the shade and slept. From the street outside came the cry of some passing pedlar, but the house was shut away from the street, not even a window pierced the brown wall; it was all turned inwards, on to the little court, private and self-contained, where the black-bearded Seyed ruled amongst his women. So it had always been in that little household, so it would continue to be through the long hot summer, when the oleander would wilt and the vine ripen its grapes on the rough supports. So it was in hundreds of little houses

Raymond Mortimer at
his morning ablutions in
the little house where the
party stayed at Kum.

all over Persia, waking in the morning; and at Dilijan, I knew, the
women would be walking up and down, below the wall, with their
twirling spindles and their long trail of wool.

Our host came out and greeted us, very tall and dark and grave,
wearing his long grey coat as though it were a robe, his beard
combed, his nails beautifully stained with fresh henna. He sat
smoking under the vine while we broke our fast. Our meal was
laid on a little ledge outside the sleeping-room: cushions of emer-
ald-green velvet, and a bunch of brilliant, single, yellow roses. A

Harold and Raymond at
breakfast in the court-
yard of the Kum house.

bowl of curdled cream. Jam in green glass jars. The brown native
bread, as crisp as a biscuit. Water in a ewer of flower-like shape.
Children came and peeped at us – small wonder, for we were the
first foreigners to cross that threshold – and the women peeped
too, holding their veils closely, and tittering; but Seyed, keeping

watch under the vine, waved them away with a lordly gesture.
Then he rose and came towards us, and invited us to follow him.

These impressions of Kum are simply like miniatures in my mind; Persian miniatures, bright, small, and sharp; intimate, enamelled. I see the arcaded background, the many figures, the ground starred with little flowers, all with the fine quality of those early paintings. Each one seems complete, as though it were already in a frame, true to itself within its own limitations, true to a general tradition also, without date, but finely classical. Seyed led us through the streets; he walked with an air of authority; we had no idea where he was taking us, nor should we have been capable of finding our way back. Through the labyrinth, between the mud walls; and already I was thinking of his house and the courtyard as of a picture seen in a book, an illumination in a missal, whose pages I had now closed, when he stopped at a door, and signed to us to enter.

Seyed had opened the book again at another illuminated page. There in the centre of the court stood the tree from which the yellow roses had been picked; a bush taller than a man, smothered in the wide, single, yellow rose that, more like a butterfly than a flower, settled upon the green. It was the magic bush of the Arabian Nights; I looked about for the Singing Fountain and the Talking Bird; a goldfish darted in the tank. Seyed stood there smiling. I realised that he was lit by some extraordinary pride; that he was showing us something that held a romantic, secret place in his life, something apart from the homeliness of his dwelling-house, a separate thing. But he made no comment, and we stood, not knowing what to say. Time hung suspended; we knew that something was about to happen, though we could not tell what; a bee blundered across the sun-warmed space; a rose broke, and the yellow petals fluttered to the ground. Then in the arches of the house, raised to the level of our eyes, appeared a young woman in a blue robe flecked with stars; she held a child in her arms. Only for an instant she appeared, framed in the arch, looking out with inquiring, expectant eyes; then as she caught sight of the strangers she gave a cry and vanished, and the court returned to its warm empty silence and the sole sentinel of the yellow rose. We looked at Seyed. He was still smiling, as a showman who for a second has drawn aside a curtain and let it fall again. Very gravely he ushered us back into the street, the door closed behind him, no remark was passed on what we had seen, we strolled towards the bazaars, talking of Russian traders on the Caspian.

III

Now that was not the last of Seyed, for, as though he deliberately intended us to learn the third aspect of his life, he led us to his shop in the bazaar. Up till then, we had not known what his profession was: we now discovered him to be a tobacconist. So completely did he reveal his life to us, with so beautiful a gravity did he disclose, in turn, the three miniatures of his existence, so authoritatively did he conduct the whole affair, that one might have suspected him of being a conscious artist. But that, of course, was out of the question. We sat in his shop, smoking and drinking tea, while the traffic of the bazaar streamed by and our merchant set forth his views on Russo-Persian relations. He was still perfectly calm and dignified, and that little interlude in the court of his secret house might never have taken place, for all the reference he made to it. He sat behind his counter, his long fingers with their orange nails idly fidgeting over the brass weights and scales, trim though noble in his appearance, a man who controlled his life. The shop was stacked from floor to ceiling with brightly coloured paper packets of cigarettes; now and then a passer-by would stop, and Seyed would rise and take down a packet, or weigh out an ounce of tobacco into a twist of paper, all with leisurely movements; and the coins he received in payment he allowed to drip from his fingers into the till as though they were of no more account to him than drops of water. It was curious to see the bazaar in this way from the opposite angle, from inside, looking out from the shop instead of looking into it. Seyed's son came, a tall dark young man, very like his father; he kept his own shop, a little way up the street. Seyed looked at him with pride. He could read; he read out a letter to his father, which Seyed had been unable to decipher. What, I wondered, was the relationship between the son and the woman in the second house? Did he even know of her existence? Did he know of it all too well? And a whole tangle of relationships presented itself to me; what communication, for instance, existed between the rather furtive, squalid women who had been sent about the business of drawing water for us, of cooking our dinner, and the blue-robed woman who had so briefly appeared behind the yellow rose, the spoilt woman, the cherished woman? Were they rivals? or mistress and servants? or, deliberately, strangers to one another? These were things which I could never know, however much they interested me; secrets which I must leave – I who drove away into a more varied life – to the sacred village and the Persian merchant.

THE CORONATION OF REZA KHAN

I

As we re-entered Teheran the sentry at the gate stopped us with the mechanical inquiry, "Az koja miayand?" "From what place do you come?" – and on receiving our reply "Az Isfahan", allowed us to proceed into the town. We found an air of excitement hanging about the streets; in the public square some tall masts, very crooked, had been set up, covered with red bunting; flags were out; festoons of electric light bulbs swooped along the façade of the municipal building. Wild, romantic horsemen paraded the

Street decorations in Teheran for the Shah's Coronation.

streets in little bunches. Triumphal arches were in process of erection. Wire silhouettes of Hercules strangling the lion, of Castor and Pollux, of aeroplanes and motor cars, gave promise of the Persians' favourite form of display: fireworks. There was no doubt about it: they had at last realised the approach of the coronation, and were bestirring themselves in a sudden, last-moment panic.

With characteristic lack of foresight they had left everything to the last, and now seemed aggrieved that because the month was

Turcoman tribesmen in Teheran for the Coronation.

Ramazan the workmen were half-hearted and languid. To hear the ministers of the court complain, you might have thought that Ramazan had come upon them unawares. Like people preparing for amateur theatricals, they were, however, sustained by the conviction that it would be all right on the day, and in the meantime they were as pleased as children with the ingenuity of their devices and with the opportunity afforded them for the exercise of their inventiveness in every form of decoration. Everything was collected together and placed on trestle-tables at intervals along the street: clocks, vases, tea-pots, photographs, china ornaments – especially clocks, for which, like most Orientals, they have a great fondness, so that the streets of Teheran tinkled all day with the strikings of discrepant hours. Then there must be illuminations; and, apart from the official lanterns and fireworks, every little household brought out its oil-lamps, its night-light glasses, and its candle-sticks, and added them to the clocks and china. Before very long, the whole of Teheran looked like an immense jumble-sale. Then, to this absurdity, was added a really effective decoration: carpets were hung against the walls of the houses, carpets closely touching, so that the mean buildings disappeared behind the arabesques of Kirman and the blood-red velvets of Bokhara. The city ceased to be a city of brick and plaster, and became a city of texture, like a great and sumptuous tent open to the sky.

Meanwhile the tribesmen continued to pour into the city. We

Kurdish tribesmen.

were not accustomed to these wild and picturesque figures; but, hung with shields and stuck with weapons, mounted on rough ponies, they sauntered down the Lazélar with a lofty disregard of the attention they attracted. Baluchis with embossed bucklers, Turcomans with great fur busbies and tunics of rose-red silk, Bakhtiaris with high white felt hats, black jackets, and white sleeves, Kurds with turbans of fringed silk; Kashgais, Lurs, Berbers, men from Sistan – these representatives of the (more or less) subject tribes composed the bodyguard of the new Shah. What with the tribes and the carpets, Teheran was losing its shoddy would-be European appearance and putting on, at last, a character more reminiscent of the pen of Marco Polo.

Down at the palace a series of works had been undertaken: the throne-room was to be repainted, the garden paved; such breaches in the walls as revealed the presence of rubbish-heaps were to be filled up; the so-called museum was to be rearranged and weeded

out. These ideas were European, and novel. The Persians themselves cared not at all whether the paint in the throne-room
betrayed patches of damp, or whether the china for the state
banquets matched, and said so quite frankly. "You see," said one
of them, "it is only recently that we have even begun to sit on
chairs." Their anxiety to impress the Europeans was endearing;
there was no point, however humble, on which they would not
consult their English friends. They would arrive with little patterns

Baluchi tribesmen.

of brocade and velvet; they would ask us to come down and
approve the colour of the throne-room. "You see," they said, "we
do not know." They ordered vast quantities of glass and china
from English firms; it would not arrive in time for the coronation,
they had left it too late, but no matter. They must have red cloth
for the palace servants like the red liveries worn by the servants at
the English legation. They must have a copy of the proceedings at
Westminster Abbey for the coronation of His Majesty George V.
The copy was procured, but, stiff with ceremonial, heavy with
regalia, created some consternation; one of the ministers who
prided himself on his English came to ask me privately what a

Rougedragon Poursuivant was, evidently under the impression that it was some kind of animal. In the amusement of the outward show of the coronation, one was apt to lose sight of the wider implications of the new regime.

To us in Teheran, Reza Khan Pahlavi, as sovereign designate, was a mysterious figure; he never showed himself except at the public salaam; never honoured any foreign mission with his presence; only occasionally, and to the dismay of the municipal auth-

orities, he would drive through unexpected parts of the city in his Rolls-Royce, after which he would send for the officials concerned, and abuse them for the bad condition of the roads. "You spend all the money on beautifying the public garden," he would say, shaking his fist angrily at the garden in question, which, in the middle of the dusty square, displayed a few yellow wall-flowers and a patch of forget-me-not behind the protection of some strands of barbed wire. He knew, of course, quite well that that was not where the money went to, and the officials knew that he knew; but the financial system of Persia is not to be altered in a day. The dictator would retire again to his private house, the officials would heave a sigh of relief, and things would go on as before. In appearance Reza was an alarming man, six foot three in height, with a sullen manner, a huge nose, grizzled hair and a brutal jowl; he looked, in fact, what he was, a Cossack trooper; but there was no denying that he had a kingly presence. Looking back, it seemed that he had risen in an amazingly short time from obscurity to his

Reza Shah on his Coronation Day with the young Crown prince, the Minister of Court, Teymourtash (centre) with the Prime Minister, Foroughi (rear left).

present position; the army was his creation and stood solid behind him; with Tamburlaine he might say,

> I am strongly mov'd
> That if I should desire the Persian crown,
> I could attain it with a wondrous ease:
> And would not all our soldiers soon consent
> If we should aim at such a dignity?

nor had he any rival in the lax limp nation he had mastered. For the ruler of Persia, however, half the problem lies precisely in the character of that nation; easy to dominate, because energy meets with no opposition, they are, once dominated, impossible to use; there is no material to build with; like all weak, soft people, they break and discourage the spirit sooner than a more difficult, vigorous race; there may be nothing to fight against, but equally there is nothing that will fight in alliance with the leader. This character leads naturally to the innumerable abuses and corruptions from which Persia suffers; the absence of justice, the sale of offices, the corruption, bribery, peculation, and general dishonesty that appals the beholder, not only from a moral point of view, but also from exasperation with the stupidity and elaboration of such a system. This internal rot, no less than the political pressure from England and Russia, must complicate the position of any energetic ruler; it is the most urgent thing, the thing which must be cleaned out before any other problem is dealt with, such problems as transport, under-population, irrigation, the condition of the peasant, the cultivation of the land.

Reza, it was said, had not desired the Persian crown, and would have preferred a republic to a kingdom, but that the priesthood insisted upon his acceptance of the throne. Not a man who cared for the outward pomps, he continued to live in his own house, and transferred himself to the palace only when he gave audience, or for some analogous purpose. The palace in question presented the most ludicrous contrasts of squalor and magnificence. The first courtyard, which from one end was dominated by the famous marble throne, was enclosed by a range of buildings resembling a gardener's bothy. Holes in the wall betrayed rubbish-heaps where the chickens scratched; the soldiers' ragged washing hung on lines stretched between the trees. A second court gave access to the garden, and to the façade of the palace; this façade was tiled, but, of course, half the tiles had fallen out, a broken-down iron railing wandered aimlessly across the terrace, the tanks were full of dead leaves, the paths muddy, half the windows smashed. A mean staircase led to the upper rooms, every step encumbered by candelabra and statues in the German taste of the mid-nineteenth century. At the top of this staircase was an enormous room, known as the museum, its walls lined with glass cases contained an

extraordinary assortment of objects, from Sassanian pottery down
to the toothbrushes of Nasred-Din Shah. This was the room —
though with its vast area of tiled floor, and its columns, and the
great height of its vaulted celing, it seemed more like a small
cathedral than a mere room — which was to be used for the
coronation ceremony, and which was then given up to workmen;
scaffolding, ladders, filled it; pots of paint stood about; the officials
were in despair; never, never, they said, would the place be cleared
by April the twenty-fifth; and then, as though the spectacle were
too distressing to contemplate any longer, they suggested a visit to
the treasury.

II

Through the garden we went, picking our way over the half-laid
bricks, while the pigeons cooed and the soft spring air wandered
in the young green of the plane trees, in an immemorial way, as
though no change of dynasty brooded over Persia; through the
garden and into the palace again, by a low doorway and a dark
narrow passage, stooping lest we should knock our heads; up a
flight of steps, reaching finally a small room with barred windows.
Knowing too well by now the shabby condition of everything in
this ramshackle country, I was not very much excited at the
prospect of seeing the treasury of imperial Iran, nor did the lacka-
daisical air of the frock-coated ministers help to raise my antici-
pations. They stood round, drinking little cups of tea, smiling
in a gentle, secret, self-satisfied way, while servants ran busily,
spreading green baize over the table, and bringing from the recesses
of an inner room leather cases and linen bags carelessly tied with
string. I was watching all this preparation with a rather perfunctory
interest, my thoughts elsewhere, when suddenly, and as with a
physical start, my eyes and thoughts came together, as gears engaging; I stared, I gasped; the small room vanished; I was Sinbad in
the Valley of Gems, Aladdin in the Cave. The linen bags vomited
emeralds and pearls; the green baize vanished, the table became a
sea of precious stones. The leather cases opened, displaying jew-
elled scimitars, daggers encrusted with rubies, buckles carved from
a single emerald; ropes of enormous pearls. Then from the inner
room came the file of servants again, carrying uniforms sewn with
diamonds; a cap with a tall aigrette, secured by a diamond larger
than the Koh-i-Nur; two crowns like great hieratic tiaras, barbaric
diadems, composed of pearls of the finest orient. The ministers
laughed at our amazement and incredulity. There seemed no end
to the treasure thus casually produced. Now at last I could believe
the story of Nars-ed-Din and his visit to the Kurds and Lurs; I
could readily have believed that he had dressed, not only himself,
but the whole of his court in just such a coruscating tabard. We
plunged our hands up to the wrist in the heaps of uncut emeralds,

and let the pearls run through our fingers. We forgot the Persia of to-day; we were swept back to Akbar and all the spoils of India.

III

The pessimism of the ministers was not justified, for on the morning of April the twenty-fifth we woke to a Teheran spruce and furbished beyond recognition. What was Reza Khan, that sulky man,

Harold Nicolson and
Raymond Mortimer
dressed for the
Coronation.

feeling on this morning of his day of supreme consummation? For my own part – since one's own part is the only part one ever truly knows – I felt quite emotionally anxious that everything should go off well; I took a personal interest in that throne-room which I had so often visited at the unofficial hour of ten in the morning, to criticise the shades of its peach-coloured distempered walls, to condemn the more outrageous of the Sèvres vases so dear to the heart of the Minister of the Court; that room which I was now about to see under its most pompous aspect, packed with dignitaries, resplendent with banners; I felt towards it much as the bride's confidential friend who right up to the hour of the ceremony has seen the bride in brogues and jersey – untidy, agitated, intimate – and now must defer, ironically, to the brocade and orangeblossom. The little heaps of dust and plaster would finally have been swept away, the carpets spread, the Peacock Throne relieved of its dust-sheets. The palace servants would no longer be in their stained blue tunics, but in the new scarlet liveries no one had yet admired. The new crown, which I had seen in the making, in sections, would be there, resplendent on a cushion. The days of being behind the scenes were over; this was the morning of the public performance.

By two-thirty we were in our places, looking down, from a raised dais, on the crowd of uniforms and frockcoats that swayed gently up and down the room. A clear space had been left down the centre, right up to the steps of the throne, that superb and barbarous divan of enamel and precious stones, tassels of rough emeralds hanging down from the arms, rubies encrusted in the back that like the spreading tail of the Indian bird rayed out before the great recess of looking-glass at the end of the room. Near the steps of the throne, to one side, shuffled and squatted and pressed

The gate of the British Legation on Coronation Day.

a crowd of mullahs; dirty, bearded old men in long robes and huge turbans; like a baleful chorus in a Greek play, they pressed forward, encroaching on the cleared space, till every now and then an aide-de-camp would be compelled to go across, and with the utmost deference whisper a request for a slight withdrawal. Black looks were obliquely cast upon the mullahs, black looks of dread and hatred as, arrogant and churlish, they conceded a yard, gathered their robes about them, and crouched back upon their haunches.

The ceremony was timed to begin at three, but half-past three still brought no sign of the opening of the doors. Owing to the presence of the mullahs, no music might be played, so it was in silence that we waited, a warm silence broken only by the whispering and rustling of the crowd. Beyond the gold lace of the

The Crown Prince in
1926 at his father's
Coronation.

diplomatic uniforms, and the light blue of the Persian officers, a
smear of richer colour stained the ranks lining the open path: an
Armenian priest in purple velvet, a Turcoman in his rose-red coat,
and, a pace in front, at intervals, stood young standard-bearers,
sheathed in chain-armour, like Crusaders mingled with the Asiat-
ics. Expectancy and imminence brooded over the crowded hall,
heightened by the silence; even the whispers about the delay were
now hushed; at last there came a stir; the doors were opened, and
the figure of a little boy appeared. Quite alone, dressed in uniform,
he marched down the length of the room, saluting, and took his
place on the lowest step of the throne, His Imperial Highness
Shahpur Mohammed Reza, Crown Prince of Persia.

Now what can be more absurd than a coronation? It argues a

veneration for kings, which no reasonable person can feel, of that primitive order which carries one back to the historical plays of Shakespeare, with their magnificent and fallacious pageantry, seductive as a child's game of make-believe; to lines of poetry in which the weight and poignancy of the line depend upon some royal word with its onerous associations. "Else a great prince in prison lies"; and why should a great prince not lie in prison, if he deserves it, as well as a simple malefactor? or the head that wears a crown not lie as uneasy as another head that boasts not even the possession of a hat? Yet in spite of all the bad thinking, and in spite of knowing it to be bad, there is that in us which revels in ceremonial, and makes us crane to see the enthronement as though we assisted indeed at some moment of august transfiguration. Escorted by his generals and his ministers bearing jewels and regalia, the aigrette in his cap blazing with the diamond known as

the Mountain of Light, wearing a blue cloak heavy with pearls, the Shah advanced towards the Peacock Throne. The European women curtsied to the ground; the men inclined themselves low on his passage; the mullahs shambled forward in a rapacious, proprietary wave; the little prince, frightened, possessed himself of a corner of his father's cloak. Only the silence seemed strange; one expected a blare of trumpets, a crashing of chords, and nothing came; only a voice droning an address, and then the voice of the Shah, reading from a paper. With his own hands he removed the cap from his head, with his own hands he raised and assumed the crown, while two ministers stood by, holding the dishonoured tiaras of the Kajar dynasty. Then from outside came a salvo of guns, making the windows rattle, proclaiming to the crowds in the

The Coronation of Reza Shah on 25 April 1926 in the throne-room of the Gulestan Palace.

streets that Reza Khan was King of Kings and Centre of the Universe.

IV

Everybody crowded out, after the Shah had gone, the ministers beaming with pleasure as they received the congratulations of their friends on the successful conduct of the ceremony. We were all much relieved, in fact, that no mishap should have come to mar the smoothness of the proceedings; that no one should have tripped over his robe or dropped a crown, or a sword, or any of the things which experience of Persia might have led us to expect. I thought, myself, that the warmth of the congratulations was perhaps a little over-emphasised, but the ministers looked innocently pleased and repeated over and over again, "Oui, en effet, tout s'est très bien passé".

Through the packed streets to the municipal building on the public square, the crowd parting to let the motors pass. The crowd seemed apathetic, a concourse of ignorant people taking very little interest in the happenings of the day; they stared dumbly, allowing the police to beat and hustle them as the English motor with the stiff little tin flag on the bonnet nosed its way amongst them. A Persian crowd is divided sharply into sexes; here a wedge of men, and there a wedge of women herded together, so that as you drive along you get first the stillness of the silent males, and then, from the black veiled figures, a sudden, charming twittering, as from a lot of birds or children. They sat cross-legged on the pavement, rising into standing tiers, peeping from under their veils; young women with bright eyes, old women like traditional mothers-in-law, tyrants of the household, and little girls holding their black snoods about them with an absurd air of grown-upness in babyhood. One never got more than a glimpse, but that glimpse revealed the whole character in a way that the uncovered face rarely does, whether it was a glimpse of the lively naughty eyes, or of the sagging, pouchy ill-tempered jowl of the old Megaera. One had brushed past them every day on the pavement, in little clusters of two and three, and caught such glimpses, but never until now seen them collected in such quantities, as though every little secret household in Teheran had poured its women out on to the pavement, jabbering, excited, on a day that would furnish a topic of conversation for a twelvemonth. Leila had seen so handsome a young Kurd, – what loins he had! – how he sat his horse! – but Zia had seen a far handsomer Englishman, – fair, tall, unlike the Persians, – what response would he make were she to send him a note? For the Persian women are very bold and enterprising under the cover of the veil, and their talk revolves always round the one single subject. Meanwhile the banners flew from the top of the crazy poles, and the wired fireworks in the middle of the square waited for night, when they would cease to look like cat's-cradle, and would flare out their brief life in pictures of red and yellow twirling fire. From the balconies of the municipal building we looked down upon the crowd, upon the route of the procession; heads blossomed at every window; the low grey building at the end of the square said IMPERIAL BANK OF PERSIA in English lettering; the clocks ticked on the trestle tables below the triumphal arches. In the distance were drawn up the detachments of the tribal bodyguard, sitting on their horses till the moment came for them to fall into their order behind the Shah's

coach. On the balconies of the municipal building, conversation flowed in safe, platitudinous channels: the new crown was of a very good design, was it not? and made by a Russian jeweller of Teheran, too! The Crown Prince was a dear little boy, was he not, with his miniature sword and his shiny boots? A horrid little boy really, said some one else; he has a violent temper and beats his servants with his fists. Glasses of lemonade were handed round, straws sticking out of them; the aspidistras on the parapet were carefully parted by gloved hands to allow the black muzzles of the kodaks to peep between. Altogether the crowning of Reza Shah provided an excellent excuse for a social occasion, both to Leila admiring the loins of the young Kurd and to Madame X. whispering confidentially to the newly arrived military attaché.

Like Cinderella, the Shah came by in a glass coach, six horses drawing him at a foot's pace, grooms with high-coloured hats like

Turcomans in the procession after the Coronation.

characters out of the ballet of Prince Igor walking beside the horses. Behind him rode his cabinet ministers, looking very ill at ease on horseback in their cashmere robes of honour; and a sullen prince of the Kajar dynasty, compelled against his will to give this public support to the usurper. Then came the Crown Prince, alone, very small, in another coach. Then the bodyguard according to their tribes, riding their horses like centaurs in full panoply; the swart barbarians of Asia. "Is it not brave to be a king, Techelles, is it

The Shah's coach in the procession.

not passing brave to be a king, and ride in triumph through Persepolis?" Not much applause greeted the Shah on his passage, for applause is not in fashion among the Persians, but a murmur travelled in his wake, and as his coach turned the corner and disappeared from sight we heard the murmur spreading up the Lalezar. When he had reached the gate of the city – but not until then – the inevitable anti-climax would take place: he would descend from his coach, remove his crown, there among the rubbish-heaps and the goats, and would re-embark in a mere motor, to be driven out to his country place. This, however, we were not privileged to see. We watched the crowd breaking up and swarming over the route of the procession, before going down ourselves and driving away to our respective homes.

V

Experience in Isfahan had been set in so different a key; the Madrasseh, the night at Kum, had imposed themselves by virtue of a quality so different and so much more elusive than this crude entertainment; it was – if so remote a parallel may be sought, – like reading Flecker after Donne, the pictorial poet after the metaphysical, the one as shallow and beguiling as the other was enriching and suggestive. Nevertheless that festive week of the coronation had its points; it was gay, it was decorative, it was absurd; the day fluttered with flags, the night dripped with gold; national anthems blared; the gems of the treasury blazed in the show-cases of the

Kurds and Bakhtiaris in the procession ride past the old town-hall, which Reza Shah was soon to replace.

coronation room, for the admiration of the officials and diplomats who thronged there evening after evening; the gardens of the palace were illuminated by coloured lanterns, that reflected in the pools, long lines of light trembling on the wrinkled surface. The Shah majestically appeared, and stood watching the fireworks, a solitary figure in his long military cloak, under the plane trees; the rockets rushed hissing upwards, hung for a second, then burst into a cluster of coloured stars; golden snakes writhed across the sky; golden showers founted and fell; an aeroplane of fire revolved its propeller, a motor-car its wheels; Castor and Pollux wrestled, Hercules overthrew the lion; golden letters jumped out of the darkness, one by one: V-I-V-E-S-A-M-A-J-E-S-T-É-I-M-P-É-R-I-A-L-P-A-H-L-A-V-I. At that, the Shah, who was standing a few paces in front of the crowd, shrugged his shoulders slightly, and, turning on his heel, made his way alone back into the palace. But for that single gesture of impatience, he had behaved in public throughout the week as an effigy, wooden and inscrutable. At many of the functions he had not even put in an appearance, but sent his son instead, who, seated in an immense scarlet tent, guarded by two soldiers with fixed bayonets, spent his time solemnly eating through the sweets piled on a table before him.

Strolling there in the palace garden, where we were now compelled to spend so many hours, I was reminded of that other Shah, Nasr-ed-Din, who in the last century used to startle Europe by his arrival in her capitals, with his Oriental accoutrements and the black moustachios like a scimitar across his face. Those were the days in which the bastinado was still a public spectacle in the streets of Teheran; when the followers of the Bab were persecuted, and the discussion about the building of a railway had just entered upon its amaranthine career; the days when a remarkable couple arrived in Teheran, and were accorded an audience with the Shah. The alley-ways of the palace garden were henceforward haunted for me by the presence of Nasr-ed-Din and the boyish figure of Jane Dieulafoy. Her husband wanted to make a study of Persian antiquities, did he? well, then, Jane would go with him, and nothing that her friends could say would dissuade her. The inducements they put forward to tempt her to remain at home were many but not various: "Un jour je rangerais dans des armoires des lessives embaumées, j'inventerais des marmelades et des coulis nouveaux; le lendemain je dirigerais en souveraine la bataille contre les mouches, la chasse aux mites, le raccommodage des chaussettes …" but, she adds, "je sus résister à toutes ces tentations." Jane Dieulafoy indeed was made of sterner stuff, and in the end it was not so much she who accompanied her husband as her husband who accompanied her. She had no illusions as to the dangers they might encounter on the way, "le moins qu'il pût nous arriver", she remarks cheerfully, "est d'être hachés en menus morceaux", and hung with scapularies, resonant with dangling and sacred medals, the prayers of their friends still ringing in their ears, they embarked for Constantinople.

A shrill February wind was blowing as the *Ava* steamed out of Marseilles. But in spite of the cold no stove was lit to warm the shivering passengers, five in number. The captain's only reply to their protests was a threat to set the punkah going, upon which they turned up the collars of their greatcoats and said no more about it. When evening came, all lights were extinguished at eight o'clock, and all matches taken away from the passengers. The reasons for these privations then transpired: the whole ship, even the passengers' private cabins, was loaded with ammunition, despatched by France to Greece for the liberation of Macedonia from Turkish rule.

Jane, however, forgot her troubles under the blue sky of Greece. It went sorely against her conscience to travel from the Piraeus to Athens "á la remorque d'une locomotive". An incurable romantic, she wanted to ride. She could not endure the idea that the smoke of an engine should soil the olive trees near the city of Pericles. But once she got up to the Acropolis she forgot the sacrilege which she had willy-nilly committed; she scrambled up the Propylea, cursed Lord Elgin, resuscitated Xerxes on his throne of gold, projected herself into the soul of the Hellenes. When she reached Constantinople her enthusiasm overflowed. Here were no trains (or at least not visible), no smoke, no coal, only slim caiques flying like arrows over the glittering waters. The Dieulafoys stayed in Constantinople for a fortnight. They saw the Sultan, howled with the howling dervishes, gyrated with the dancing dervishes, ate kebabs and cheese pastry, explored the bazaars, and were informed that the best road into Persia lay *via* Tiflis.

Now March is not the ideal month to choose for journeying over the roads of this difficult country. As I have already said, and say again in print, since we, living there, said it in speech a dozen times a week: if the weather is mild, the snows melt; if it is severe, they do not, so the traveller has to take his choice between floods or snowdrifts. After innumerable adventures the Dieulafoys finally reached Kasvin, and a mere hundred miles lay between them and the capital. They had already been three months on the way, they had covered over six hundred kilometres of bad roads, their coach had overturned several times, they had been compelled to spend stormy nights in the open, they had run the gauntlet of Kurdish brigands. Jane was not afraid of brigands, but inclined rather to the belief that they were afraid of her. "Je me considère avec orgueil. Se peut-il qu'un gamin de ma taille épouvante les Kurdes, ces farouches nomades?" All these adventures successfully surmounted, the 9th of May saw them at Kasvin, but here a real misfortune overtook them: Monsieur Dieulafoy fell ill. Jane was indomitable. She procured a waggon, but where were the horses? Jane scoured Kasvin for horses, and found them at three o'clock in the morning. The suffering Marcel was laid in the waggon on a mattress; they rumbled out of the town, but before they had gone five miles the wheels sank in mud; they were stuck. Jane herself seized the reins and thrashed the team. Peasants came to the rescue with oxen. Somehow or other they made their way along the execrable road and by nightfall were no more than twenty miles from the capital. Here the toll-keeper refused to allow them to continue. But Jane had seen the snowy cone of Demavend like a white beacon ahead, and over-rode all his objections. By ten o'clock that night, with Marcel delirious in the waggon, they pulled into Teheran.

Here for three weeks Jane remained at the invalid's bedside, never once going beyond the gate of the hotel garden, which for a creature of her energetic and inquiring disposition at least gives proof of a very considerable devotion. Early in June, frail, tottering, but convalescent, Marcel was led out to have an audience of the Shah. Under the charge of the French doctor, the Dieulafoys awaited his Majesty in the garden of the palace, having first rammed their hats firmly on their heads, lest they should inadvertently remove them in the imperial presence (was this Jane's habitual gesture of salutation?), "ce qui serait de la dernière grossièreté". Presently Nasr-ed-Din, followed by his servants, was seen approaching between the trees; an interpreter walked beside him, reading aloud from a French newspaper; the Shah wore a black fez, a cashmere robe, white drill trousers, pumps, white socks, and white cotton gloves on his small hands. Jane was impressed by his distinguished appearance, his hooked nose, his white teeth, black hair, and moustachios. The party bowed deeply, and the doctor begged leave to present Monsieur and Madame Dieulafoy.

"What", said the Shah, "is that boy a woman?" On being assured that it was so, he addressed Jane in French. Why, he enquired, was she not dressed in the long skirts and garments of European ladies? Jane replied that she found man's dress more convenient, and that a European woman travelling in Mohammedan countries was too much exposed to an inconvenient curiosity. "True", said the Shah, "but do you suppose that if a Persian woman in her veil appeared on the Paris boulevards, she would not immediately become the centre of a large crowd? Can you paint?" he asked abruptly. Jane said no, she could not. "That's a pity", said the Shah; "I should have liked a portrait of myself on horseback. Do you know Grévy? do you know Gambetta? how is Grévy?" he said to Marcel. "How old are you?" he asked, without waiting for answers. Marcel said he was thirty-seven. "You look a great deal older," said the Shah. "Don't forget to tell Monsieur Grévy I am his good friend," and the audience was over.

Then the Dieulafoys must take the road again, with Marcel recovered; that Isfahan road, and the farther road which I did not know: the road to Shiraz, Persepolis, Fars, Susa. Before them lay experiences both pleasant and unpleasant; the midsummer sun to be faced over stretches of shadeless plain; the feverish swamps of the Karoun River. Cold, flood, and mud they had overcome between Tabriz and Teheran; now they must endure the worst heats of summer, scorching or malarial. "I would not", said Jane, "wish my enemy such pleasures. That he should follow the English telegraph line from Teheran to Shiraz I would allow; but may his evil star never lead him into Fars, into Kousistan, or to the cursed banks of the Karoun."

Between Teheran and Shiraz, indeed, the journey went smoothly forward; we get glimpses of Jane, on her passage through Persian villages, playing "La Fille de Madame Angot" on the harmonium to local governors (but she played it too fast for their taste, and had to play it again, half time); explaining to Persian ladies that

The Koran Gate, Shiraz.

Queen Victoria has no beard, and only one husband; falling asleep on her horse from weariness at the end of the day. But when they plunged again into Persia (after an excursion into Iraq), into the wild provinces, bound for Susa, it is a different story. Jane fell so ill with fever that fragile objects were no longer to be entrusted to her shaking hands. Yet she would not turn back. Day after day she rode, strapped to her horse lest she should fall; and though sometimes she thought her strength would give out before the caravan reached its destination, her enthusiasm always revives as tomb or ruin comes into sight; she is always ready to draw the ground-plan for Marcel; always ready to listen to the songs of the itinerant musician they have carried along with them on the way. Her health might fail, but her spirit never. Even on the boat, bound at last for France after a long year's journey, shattered by fever, no sooner has her strength recovered enough to let her walk from one end of the deck to the other without undue exhaustion, than she seizes her pen again and reviews the entire history of Persia. Jane returned to France a celebrated woman. But she had paid the price. The pleasure of relating her adventures cost her two hundred grains of quinine; and though she was willing to overlook the chemist's bill, she bore a long grudge for her broken health and her failing eyesight.

But it was not so much of Jane on her travels that I thought, as of Jane in the Teheran of the early 'eighties, and of the great pity that she could not paint Nasr-ed-Din on horeback, for her diary would certainly have chronicled their conversations as their acquaintance progressed, with Jane standing peremptory behind her easel and the Shah reining in his mount, two people both accustomed to say what they meant, both no doubt giving as good as they got, beneath the plane trees of the garden, in the sun and shadows of a Persian June. Time, I found, passed very pleasantly for me in the elaboration of these scenes which had never taken place; it was a pleasanter occupation than listening to the platitudes of the acquaintances with whom I paced the walks, in the uncertain swaying of the coloured lights. Then suddenly I heard the words of my companion of the moment chime in with my secret game: "Yes", the voice was saying reminiscently, "I remember that as a child in Paris I was once allowed to be present at an evening party. My father, holding me by the hand, told me to look at the person who had just come into the room. I looked, and saw a little grizzled old gentleman, in a smoking-jacket, with the Legion of Honour in his buttonhole. 'That', said my father, 'is Madame Dieulafoy'."

CHAPTER IX

RUSSIA

I

THE countryside had also decked itself for the coronation; all along the roads, where the judas trees had now shed their magenta and clothed themselves in leaf instead, the jasmine and wild roses were in full flower. In the gardens, poor stunted tea-roses that in England would have been torn up by a derisive hand and flung on the bonfire, had for some weeks past been putting forth their blooms; but it is for the exuberance of the native wildling that one must wait before one understands the reputation of Persian roses. Huge bushes, compact, not straggling like the English dog-rose, spattered with flame-coloured blossom; the ground carpeted with fallen petals – this is the first impression, then a closer scrutiny reveals the lovely shape of the separate flower, the pure, early shape of the briar-rose, of a pristine simplicity which our whorled hybrids, superlative though they be, can never excel; and, allied to that early, naked design, a colour such as all our cross-fertilisation fails to produce: the interior of the petal red, but lined with gold, the two together giving a glow of orange, a burning bush. Side by side with these grew the yellow rose, which to me was always the rose of Kum, and the low, shrubby jasmine, and plumes of acacia that scented the air; the brief spring was once more making the most of its allotted season. I could not believe but that the earth was ready to break into other sudden, concealed riches, for I had learnt by now to take nothing on trust, and to ignore the disparagements of other people, for very quickly I had discovered that those who found 'nothing to see' were those who did not know how to look; but although equipped with this pharisaical humour, I might no longer indulge it, for the time had come for me to return to England.

Already the promise of summer hung over Persia; the planes were heavy in leaf, and the trickle of water became more persistent, as the gardeners (with one trouser leg rolled up to the thigh, a fashion I could never wholly explain) released the pent-up streams and allowed them to pour over the thirsty beds, or padded bare-footed about the garden, splashing water to lay the dust in the early morning. We no longer courted the sun, but darkened the house all day with reed blinds, raising them only in the evening when the snows of Demavend turned red, and the dusk came quickly, and the little owls began to hoot, and the frogs hopped on the garden path, and the breeze rose and sighed in the planes. The imminence of departure oppressed me; I was beginning to say,

"This time next week ..." and to suffer when I heard people making plans for a date, not very far distant, when I should no longer be there; heartlessly they made their plans, the people for whom life flowed continuous, while I sat by and listened, under sentence of death; then the days began to rush, and the day came which was still an ordinary day for other people, but for me was a day so different. An early start, so like, so unlike, the start for Isfahan; the motor at the door; luggage being carried out; the curtained windows of other houses, whose inhabitants still slept, would sleep for three hours longer, by which time I should be sixty miles away; the early morning life just stirring, the white pony going his rounds with the water-casks; a freshness over everything; the dogs wanting to come; being refused; the servants wishing me a good journey, and bringing me little presents; the fat cook coming out in his white shoes with a basket of little cakes. My room empty upstairs, but my books still on the shelves; my handwriting, reversed, still on the blotting-paper; good-bye, good-bye; for Heaven's sake let us get this over. The guard at the gate saluting, then the streets, the Kasvin gate, the Kasvin road; what a difference, between arrival and departure! *then*, everything had been new, I had looked with curiosity, Demavend himself had had to be pointed out to me and named, I had not known what to expect next round the turn of the road; *now*, everything was a landmark to be left behind, every place had a meaning and an association; there was the shop where we had bought the pots, there was the place of meeting for the paper-chase, there was the track that led up to Var-dar-Var, where we had first found the wild almond in flower, and had marked off an unknown shrub with a ring of stones. Still the donkeys trailed along the road, though camels were few, for they had gone up to Gilan for the spring grazing; and every one I met going towards Teheran I envied; and every one I overtook going towards Kasvin I pitied for being in the same plight as I.

After Kasvin the road was unfamiliar, and the character of the landscape changed with surprising abruptness. We were no longer on the roof; the high, arid plateaus were gone; the vegetation became lush and green, the climate changed from the clear air of four thousand feet to the mild, steamy atmosphere of sub-tropical sea-level. We had dropped from over four thousand feet in a few hours, down a precipitous road into the valley of the White River. The scenery was fine, in its way; groves of trees descended the steep slopes to the banks of the river, and between the trees could be seen green meadows, as green as Devonshire, with cows peacefully grazing or − an odd effect − camels grazing in this Devonshire landscape, as who should come upon a herd of camels in the meadows above the Dart; the valley of the White River had its beauty, but it was not Persia as I understood it, and I resolved that I would never bring any one into Persia for the first time by that road, but would subject them to the rigours of the plains and passes of Kermanshah and Hamadan. Evening fell; we seemed to have been travelling interminably; the continual hairpin corners made driving very tiring; we met strings of hooded waggons, whose miserable teams could scarcely drag them up the hill; men were shouting, and tugging at the bridles, and thrashing the stumbling horses; we got past them all somehow, and drew up in a village by the river where a notice-board proclaimed the Hotel Fantasia.

It was well named, for a crazier building I never saw; an outside staircase, with two steps missing, led up to a wooden balcony, and here we pitched our camp-beds and slept as well as the fleas would allow us. There had been no fleas at Dilijan or at Kum; the rooms there had been bare and clean; it was typical of the difference between that happy and this miserable journey. There, we had gone to sleep conscious of the free space all around us; here, we were in a narrow valley with the river roaring in a brown flood fifty yards away, and no sense of Asia. Next day the road ran on into the fertile Gilan, chestnut woods appeared, olives, and fields of rice; the country was flat, the young rice of a brilliant green

indescribable to those who have not seen it; even the peasants walked with a different gait, because from childhood they must pick their way, carrying baskets slung from either end of a long pole across their shoulders, along the narrow ridges dividing rice-swamp from rice-swamp, a characteristic celebrated in the local

Traffic on the road from Teheran to Resht, where Vita said goodbye to Harold.

poetry; out of the flooded fields rose little Chinese-looking shelters built on piles, in which the peasants keep watch at night for wild pig; the houses were no longer of mud, but of brick, tiled or thatched like cottages in Hampshire; where was my Persia gone? and I imagined how this road would seem, coming the other way, into Persia instead of out; how after following the valley along its course, and climbing up, up, instead of going down, down, the traveller would suddenly find himself on the table-land heights, with the grandeur suddenly revealed to him. But we came to Resht, a brown-red town that had nothing in common with the sun-dried villages I knew, and, remorselessly carried onward, next day I realised that I was on the Caspian, and that the fading mountains on the horizon were the last I should see of Persia.

Then little by little every link that still bound me to Persia began to drop away; I lost the direction of Teheran, my watch no longer registered Teheran time, my Persian cigarettes gave out and were replaced by Russian ones. By such small things did I realise my severance. Then a fog came down, hiding the line of the Elburz, and the little steamer hooted her mournful way across the sea, and morning dawned upon the coast of Russia.

II

I had been prepared to enter into an atmosphere of gloom and fear; all my sensibility was on the alert to receive such an impression; but I cannot say that in Baku I experienced anything of the sort. Perhaps the Russians of the south are by temperament gayer than the people of the north, for certainly the citizens of Baku have seen their share of trouble, both in their own town and in the neighbouring Caucasian provinces – twenty-five people, so I was told, had been shot in Baku itself on the previous day, – yet one heard singing in the streets, people laughed and looked merry, wore bright colours, made love on the benches in the public garden. Lack of trains compelled me to spend two days at Baku; the hotel was good, the food excellent, the caviare of course fresh and abundant, the hotel servants civil and obliging. I had expected to be crowded off the pavement into the street; not a bit of it. I was almost disappointed. Was this Bolshevik Russia? There was nothing to show me what country I was in except the notices written in Russian, the belted blouses of the men, and the padded blue cab-drivers sitting behind their yoked horses. After Persia, the first thing which struck one was the general air of prosperity; it was extraordinary to see houses of stone, paved streets, electric trams, and the great well-fed horses with their rounded rumps; though perhaps coming the other way, from Europe, it would not have been so remarkable. The first hint I had of anything different was at Baku station; arrived there, with our tickets and papers all in order, we (that is to say, myself and some Persian friends whom

I had fortunately met) were informed that no places could be reserved in advance. The train came from Tiflis; was always crowded; we had very little chance of finding room. There would be another train in four days' time.... It was lucky that my acquaintances knew Russian, or I might be at Baku to this day. The Persian Consulate-General was called by telephone; some official or other promised that the impossible should be done; meanwhile we were put with our luggage into what had once been the Imperial waiting-room, and which was now decorated with enlarged photographs of Chicherin and Litvinoff, and with a bust of Lenin draped in scarlet and black. In this waiting-room (which, although stripped of its magnificence so far as possible, still betrayed its Imperial origin in the luxury of its separate entrance and its adjoining lavatories) some miscellaneous persons beside ourselves were herded: some peasant women with bundles, and a shabby little man who sat huddled on a divan, and who, we were warned, had been put there to listen to our conversation. For the first time we dropped our voices and guarded our words – an unpleasant sensation, but one destined to become familiar. Presently the train steamed into the station; we began to agitate; a railway official came in and said with a wink that a carriage was being 'cleaned out' for us; this, it appeared, was a euphemistic way of saying that its occupants were being turned out and left to shift for themselves for our benefit – again, not my idea of Bolshevik Russia.

Most people have the idea that travelling in Russia is to-day almost out of the question; they know vaguely that the classes are no longer called 'first' and 'second', but 'soft' and 'hard'; this frightens them, and they do not stop to reflect that it comes to exactly the same thing. Let me assure them that Russian trains are quite as comfortable as European trains; in fact, rather more comfortable, for they go very slowly and run on a wider gauge. For a few roubles you can hire pillows, blankets, and sheets, perfectly clean and supplied to you in a sealed sack. You are also given a towel, but no water to wash with. To compensate for the absence of water, the trains are usually run on wood, which does away with the peculiar grime of coal-driven railways. There is really nothing to complain of. But for some reason – connected, I suspect, with the question of commissions on the sale of tickets – if you go to a travelling agency in London and ask for a ticket to Teheran via Moscow, you will be met with a pitying smile and the word 'Impossible'.

There is nothing further to be said in favour of the journey from Baku to Moscow, for it is exceedingly monotonous; the names of the Caucasus, the Sea of Azov, Rostov-on-Don seemed full of suggestion, but it very quickly evaporated: the Caucasus was reduced to a few foothills, the Sea of Azov looked much like any other sea, and of Rostov one sees only the railway station, unrelieved even by the presence of a Don Cossack. After Rostov the steppe begins, and 'le long ennui de la plaine'; very different from the Persian plains, it rolls away to the horizon in green billows, not arid enough to be impressive, not luxuriant enough to be beautiful, dotted with poor Cossack villages, populated by drab peasants. A sad country. Then we passed through the Ukraine, which depressed me in spite of its rich black soil, for I remembered how before the war I had stayed there in the magnificent hospitality of Polish friends, riding, dancing, laughing; living at a fantastic rate in that fantastic oasis of extravagance and feudalism, ten thousand horses on the estate, eighty English hunters, and a pack of English hounds; a park full of dromedaries; another park, walled in, full of wild animals kept for sport; Tokay of 1750, handed round by a giant; cigarettes handed round by dwarfs in eighteenth century liveries; and where was all that now? Gone, as it deserved to go; the house razed to the ground till it was lower than the wretched hovels of the peasants, the estate parcelled out, cut in half by the new Polish frontier, the owner dead, with his brains blown out, and his last penny gambled away in Paris. I had not realised that we should pass so near.

III

On the third day we arrived at Moscow. I scarcely know how to write of Moscow; I have only that to say which others have said before, others who have had a longer and more privileged experience than I, and who even so have not succeeded in finding any definition. I was in Moscow a very short time, I spoke with very few Russians; yet I felt that if I were condemned to live there for long I should go mad. Why, exactly, I felt this, I cannot say; I do not think it was suggestion, or I should surely have felt the same at Baku; besides, by the time I arrived in Moscow, I was inclined to pooh-pooh the accounts I had heard of the 'depressing atmosphere of Russia'. It is a fixed idea, I had said to myself in Baku, this depressing atmosphere; people feel it because they think they ought to feel it, but there is no evidence of it anywhere. What made it the more alarming was that no actual evidence of it existed in Moscow either; but when you enter a room in which two people have just been having an emotional scene, you are aware of the atmosphere at once, even though they control themselves in your presence; so it was with Moscow. Nothing visible happened, yet the air was charged; and tiny indications corroborated. People glanced over their shoulders at dinner to see whether the servants were listening; conversation became freer when the servants had left the room; dinner-parties were given indeed, but every guest arrived rather as though he had just escaped a lion in the street. But I was convinced not so much by these things, in private houses,

Moscow, the Red Square.

nor by the furtive confidences poured out to a complete stranger by fellow-guests – tales of false money slipped into pockets, and arrests made on that formal charge – as by my own intuition and the aspect of the town. I know that intuition is a poor argument; I know that it is presumptuous to touch even the fringe of the Russian problem without cognizance, economical, political, historical, of all the facts; but what of Kinglake's traveller, who tells of all objects, not as he knows (or does not know) them to be, but as they seem to him? For all I know, it may be true that a great spirit of elation informs the Russian people; all I can say is, that if Moscow is an elated city, then let me live elsewhere. I got the impression of a population furtively slinking along the walls; a people cowering away; a nation whose aspirations had been trimmed to a dead level, as a hedge. There was beggary, the depth to which one might sink; but no height, beyond that dead level, to which one might rise. And yet again, I do not know. Possibly the judgement is warped from the start because one instinctively applies the ordinary standards of Western Europe to this country which has discarded the dominant Western conception – that of Wealth as the be-all and end-all of existence – without yet achieving the peace and freedom in which the new ideals may develop. That is to say, the general aspect of poverty in Moscow – the fact that no one dresses better than his neighbour – may have much, too much, to do with our hasty conclusions. We are too well accustomed to associate material prosperity with spiritual happiness. So, also, we are too impatient, we who have grown up in a country where change, although it seems quick to us, is a mere tortoise

Red Square, Moscow, in 1926. A tourist photograph which Vita picked up during her one-day visit.

compared with such volcanic overthrows; we are too impatient, too intolerant of disorder, even temporary, to allow for the difficult and painful stage of transition; we like settled things, established things; we will not realise that the personal freedom which we demand as our right, and whose mildest infringement we resent, cannot exist as yet under a young system, dangerous, precarious, grappling on to its existence. Communism is fighting for its life, it is unscrupulous, brutal, criminal; it forces us to say that the Russians have but exchanged one tyranny for another; but, however much we may blame it for its methods, we cannot say that it is, *in its aims*, immoral. Taking a God's-eye view, what possible redemption can we suggest for the world but an escape from materialism? And that is what Soviet Russia would enforce. It may be an impossible ideal. To enforce it leads to barbarism, persecution, misery, cant, and to the questionable practice of underhand interference with other countries; but all this does not alter the idea which lies, sound, at the root of the matter. The practical difficulties may prove too great, the mercenary, predatory instincts of human nature too strong; for, in common with that other great idea, a league of nations, Communism has human nature as an opponent. To overcome this, the Soviet would say in self-justification, human nature must be crushed, coerced; it must be altered, willy-nilly; it must be reborn. Small wonder that a people undergoing the process of such coercion should slink along the walls of the capital as malefactors dreading the descent of the hand of justice. Conform and live; dissent and die.

IV

That was a curious journey home, its beginning in personal heart-sickness, its middle in intense, impersonal interest, its end in sheer farce. For, when the train reached the Polish frontier, at dawn, after a night spent in the 'hard' class with three Russians, strangers, – a night during which I revised my ideas of Russian travelling, – and when every one in the train was sighing with relief, and saying "Thank goodness, we arrive in civilised Europe again", we were met with quite other news. Revolution in Poland; Warsaw in the hands of the rebels; the telegraph wires cut; the line blown up; no trains able to proceed to Warsaw. The dismayed passengers crowded round the phlegmatic officials in the customs shed. No, they could tell us nothing more; the train would go on as far as it could, perhaps to within twenty, perhaps fifteen miles of Warsaw; there we should be turned out and left to our own devices; people were being shot down in the streets of Warsaw; how many? perhaps three hundred, perhaps three thousand; who could tell? No news was coming through. Would they advise us to go on or not? They shrugged, they could not advise; if we liked to risk it . . . I was not afraid of being shot, but I *was* afraid of being indefinitely delayed.

A mixed company of Germans, Russians, and Austrians, who were afraid of the same thing, finally sorted themselves out from the babbling crowd of passengers, and drifted into a little group apart, as people will, whose interests and opinions are the same, in even the tiniest and most newly born of communities. I found myself with eight or nine middle-aged, bullet-headed men, who looked, roughly speaking, like commercial travellers; and one blonde, very blonde, young woman, an Austrian, travelling in the company of one of the men, in what capacity it was not hard to determine. A time-table was produced from somewhere; assuming that it still held good for the unaffected parts of Poland, we calculated that we should be able to reach the German frontier that night. The Germans had but one idea in their heads, and that was to sleep that night in their own country. Considering the rumours that were current – the whole of Poland under military rule within twenty-four hours, railways and bridges destroyed, communication with the rest of Europe interrupted – I could scarcely blame them; indeed, I shared their determination. My difficulty was that I had no money. I had my ticket through from Moscow to London, and only enough cash to pay for my food on the way: how was I to buy new tickets, however 'hard' I might be prepared to travel? A fellow-passenger came to my rescue. He was a shabby little man, dressed in a ready-made suit, his hair *en brosse*, but he produced from his pocket-book wads of American notes, which he pressed into my hand. For once the orange labels on my luggage had served a useful purpose. There they hung, in the restaurant of the Polish station, crumpled, defaced, but still saying: PERSIA. Alas, Persia was very far away; I had now been travelling for twelve days; it seemed sufficiently absurd that I should have come out of Asia only to run into a revolution in Europe. Still, I was amused rather than annoyed; amused to find myself in the company of these unknown units, all linked together, suddenly, by a common predicament, familiarly talking together, although the whole background of our lives remained an unknown quantity. Herr Müller, Herr Rosendorf; I picked up their names little by little.

The train took us as far as Bialystok; there we were left uncertain on the platform; some one suggested a motor, some one else an aeroplane; but the problem was solved for us by the arrival of a small, local train, which would at any rate put us a little farther on our way. In this we proceeded at a very leisurely pace all day, crawling round the back of Poland, seeing no sign of revolution except a few troops standing about at country stations, and a few sentries posted near bridges and signal-boxes. It was warm, and the corn was growing; the farm and homesteads looked prosperous, not unlike English farms; it was pleasant to come back to spring, after Russia where the spring had not yet broken, and to see rural Poland thus unexpectedly, instead of keeping to the beaten track.

It was a rolling landscape, with clumps of dark firs on the sky-line, well-kept roads, gates painted a clean white; after Persia and Russia, I felt that I was really back in Europe. At eight o'clock, after this peaceful and uneventful journey, we arrived at a small frontier town – Grajevo. Out on the platform again, and into another customs shed, only to learn that the train would go no farther. And what about the trains next day? Oh, the trains next day, said the Poles, there probably wouldn't be any trains next day. My Germans were in consternation. Sleep on Polish soil they would not. Were there any motors? Yes, there was one motor in Grajevo, but it was broken down. But there was an engine in the siding; could we not have that? Well, said the Poles very dubiously, we might perhaps have that, but not until one o'clock in the morning, not until all was quiet and everybody gone to bed. After some consultation we closed with this offer. It remained only for us to put away the hours between eight and one.

A postcard of Gravejo, Poland, close to the German frontier, where Vita and her fellow-fugitives providentially escaped a revolution.

There is not much to do in a Polish village. We wandered out into the street, the Germans now a hilarious band, arm-in-arm, singing student songs, since they saw some prospect of escape; but it was obvious that we could not walk up and down for half the night, even so mild a night, under the stars, in the dark street. I wondered what my friends in England would say if they could miraculously see me, instead of thinking of me comfortably asleep in a *wagon-lit*, rushing across Europe? For Polish revolutions mean very little to us when we read the headlines in the morning paper, but when you run into them they lead you, as I was finding, into unusual situations.

> Nach Frankreich zogen zwei Grenadier',
> Die waren in Russland gefangen,

sang the Austrian blonde in a rich contralto, and laid her golden head on the shoulder of her companion. Everybody was very good-humoured and merry. Then some one espied a café, with a light showing, and we burst noisily in there, and were established round a table in a little room, a cottage piano in one corner, and on the walls coloured lithographs of Millais' Angelus and of a Russian sledge being pursued by wolves. In the next room, some Polish officers, sitting drinking at little tables, eyed us curiously, as well they might. Herr Rosendorf called for wine; he called for vodka; both were brought, and bacon and eggs, and the table laid in a twinkling. The vodka dwindled in the bottle; the party became

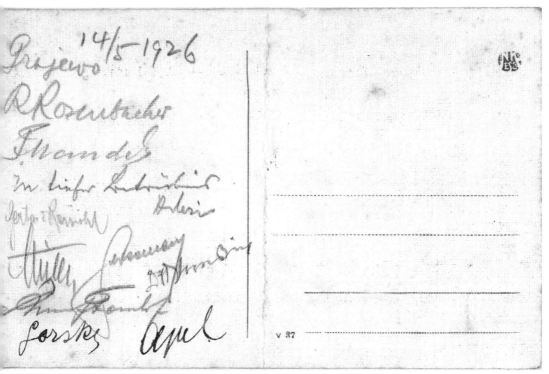

Signatures of Vita's multinational companions.

uproarious. German, Russian, and English were spoken indifferently, and even a few words of Japanese by somebody just returning from Japan. Everybody shouted little bits of information about themselves. My opposite number leaned across the table and announced to me, in a stentorian voice, "I have travelled Singer's sewing machines one hundred thousand miles over Manchuria". "Say something in Persian," they demanded, and I repeated a verse from Hafiz. These middle-aged, bullet-headed gentlemen became as children; they even beat on the table with spoons. Then one of the Polish officers, unable to bear his isolation any longer, came in and started playing the 'Blue Danube' on the piano. The Austrian blonde sprang up and began to dance. The men quarrelled in an arch, skittish way as to who should dance with her, pushing each other about, and digging one another in the ribs: chairs were overturned; somebody made a speech; post-cards were bought, and passed round for everybody's signature. By this time they were all very drunk indeed. The Austrian blonde shook off her partner, returned to her place, laid her head on her arms and began to cry. Her companion sat stroking her hair, a pleased smile on his face. She nestled, kittenish, into his arms and went to sleep.

She woke up, however, at the first movement towards departure, pulled out a little mirror, attended to her face, combed her short golden hair, and, pouting, allowed herself to be escorted into the street. There, at the station, was our engine, with a tender attached, puffing red clouds into the night; we climbed aboard amongst many jokes and much hilarity, suppressed by the railway officials, who kept glancing anxiously and guiltily round. As we steamed off, down the dark line, nothing could restrain the party; they sang 'Deutschland über Alles'; remembered my presence; stopped; said they hoped England did not mind: so England was compelled to join in. Thus we came into Germany.

V

I forget the name of the German village; I know only that I had three hours sleep in a clean little room with an iron bedstead and a blue tin basin, and that we were all in a train again by six the next morning. That day passed in a haze: Königsberg; a long wait there, drinking coffee out of thick cups and looking at photographs in the German papers of the scenes in Warsaw; then another train; the Polish Corridor; East Prussia; Berlin. Farewell to my companions, who were to scatter to their destinations. The efficiency of Berlin; the quick, good taxi, striped black and white like a bandbox; the lighted streets; the polished asphalt; the Kaiserhof. I was travel-stained and tired; the servants at the Kaiserhof looked at me with polite suspicion; I revenged myself on them by sending for the head waiter, ordering the best dinner and the most expensive wine, and by distributing enormous tips out of my wad of American notes. As I had not had a proper meal since leaving Moscow, I took a good deal of trouble over the ordering of that dinner. I was afraid I might have to spend the night in Berlin, but I discovered a train that left for Flushing at ten; next morning found me in Holland. The customs-house officer at the Dutch frontier made me an offer of marriage. Then everything began to rush. Was I on the sea? very rough, too; beautiful, green, white-crested waves; was I at Folkestone? with English voices talking round me? was that Yew Tree Cottage and the path across the fields? Were those the two pistons at Orpington, still going up and down, and still a little wrong? Was I standing on the platform at Victoria, I who had stood on so many platforms? The orange labels dangled in the glare of the electric lamps. PERSIA, they said; PERSIA.

A storyteller, Isfahan.